The Work of Creation

The Work of Creation

Selected Prose

Luke Hankins

WIPF & STOCK · Eugene, Oregon

THE WORK OF CREATION
Selected Prose

Wipf & Stock
An Imprint of Wipf and Stock Publishers
199 W. 8th Ave., Suite 3
Eugene, OR 97401

www.wipfandstock.com

ISBN 13: 978-1-4982-8652-7

Manufactured in the U.S.A.   11/30/2015

Also by Luke Hankins

Poetry:

Weak Devotions (Wipf & Stock, 2011)

As editor:

Poems of Devotion: An Anthology of Recent Poets
(Wipf & Stock, 2012)

As translator:

I Was Afraid of Vowels . . . Their Paleness (Q Avenue Press, 2011)
poems from the French of Stella Vinitchi Radulescu

Praise for *The Work of Creation*

In his generous and illuminating volume of prose, *The Work of Creation*, Luke Hankins demonstrates how much of poetry and the maturation of our engagement with it rely upon a power to contain opposites, particularly as they problematize our historical moment. With the wide-angle of a theorist and the jeweler's monocle of a close reader, the author here sets out to revalidate and reposition the poet's work as part of a more fundamental set of contemporary challenges: to seek the genuine in the fractured, divine union in uncertainty, magnanimity in despair—and thus to forge greater intimacies among aesthetics, ethics, and psychology. In praise of the devotional, the book honors a radiance of doubt that eschews both easy ironies and dogmatic polemics. The subtext here is gratitude, a love of work, and a deepening summons to the complexity of art as bound to the complexity of our condition. A beautiful book.

—**Bruce Bond**, author of *Immanent Distance: Poetry and
the Metaphysics of the Near at Hand*

This collection is tuned to the pitch of listening—listening with fine intelligence as Hankins explores the nuances of poetry, culture, and history: the soul.

—**Claire Bateman**, author of *Leap* and *Scape*

Praise for *Weak Devotions*

It is appropriate to call Luke Hankins' powerful, surprising first collection of poems, *Weak Devotions*, "confessional," but with an emphasis on the original religious sense of the word. These poems are not in any way self-absorbed or self-pitying, but, like in the *Confessions* of Saint Augustine and Rousseau, they are written out of a commitment to an ideal of self-scrutiny. These poems are not "clever": although their tonal range is excitingly broad, including Miltonic high diction, the colloquial immediacy of Beat poetry, and the conversational clarity of Elizabeth Bishop, one tone which is not heard in them is irony. They are honest. Selfhood is not dramatized in narcissistic display, but is present everywhere in language-acts of integrity. These poems are decisive, grounded in particulars of place, experience and intellect, and courageously engaging of the reader, who is addressed as a fellow human being trying, like the poet, to live well, and looking for the imagination for help with that task. These poems do help.

—**Christopher Davis**, *Connotation Press*

Luke Hankins' poetry shimmers with intellect and craft. However, what is most surprising about it, especially in our time, is that it wrestles with the issues Donne, Herbert, Hopkins, Vassar Miller, and countless others also found worthy of their most impassioned work. Hankins' voice, which, even in the midst of a religious meditation, can be irreverent and secular, is neither out of date nor irrelevant to the lives of millions. But one need not be religious to be moved by poetry as finely wrought as is found in his brilliant title poem and elsewhere in this book.

—**John Wood**

There is great compassion in these poems, most especially for the vicissitudes of childhood, when the mystery of life is first unfolding. But Hankins understands that "there are few words left sufficient to this world" to explain or console or lift up as praise, and that even the loveliest poem may prove a weak devotion. Still, Hankins does not give in to uncertainty or despair. Rather, in masterfully wrought poems, he exhorts us to "abandon ideas and concepts of beauty" and "be part of it," a natural and blessed part of life's great dance. In the beautiful poem "Wisteria," the poet convinces us that it is in fact possible to give oneself over to the mysterious "sweetening sun," like a vine-wrapped tree that becomes "what rises through it." Such brave surrender is, I think, what gives these heartfelt poems their clarity, power, and grace.

—**Richard Jones**, *editor of Poetry East*

Praise for *Poems of Devotion: An Anthology of Recent Poets*

Hankins makes a determined, refreshingly testy attempt to define what devotional poetry is, and what it is not, in an introductory essay [. . .]. [T]his collection's central accomplishment [is that] it shows in no uncertain terms that devotional poetry continued throughout the 20th century and into the 21st [. . .]. [. . .] Even more exciting, however, is a second impression fully felt only toward the end of the book—that devotional poetry not only abides in the present century but is positively thriving these days, showing promise for the future. [. . .] *Poems of Devotion* bears an exciting message, then, and one that any anthology that includes very current work would covet: "Times are good." Hankins ends his collection on a high note as well, remarking in [a] concluding interview, "We make because we are made. We are made because God loves to make. We are the result of the pleasurable work of the divine." That is beautifully said, and for readers who think so, too, they would do well to seek out Hankins' own collection of poetry, *Weak Devotions*, recently released.

—**Brett Foster**, *Books & Culture*

The phrase "contemporary devotional poetry" is more likely to conjure images of treacly holiday greeting cards than literature of the highest order. But this anthology, on the contrary, bears witness to the perennial human desire to adore—and to question, Job-like—the Almighty. This is a generous and inclusive selection, containing not only modern masters but also emerging voices. Above all, it is a reminder that the best writing is, in the end, an offering to the Mystery.

—**Gregory Wolfe**, *editor of Image*

Praise for *I Was Afraid of Vowels . . . Their Paleness*

Like seashells with light shining through, these poems by Stella Vinitchi Radulescu express the tough fragility of being; in his lucid translation, Luke Hankins mirrors perfectly their deftness and their strength.

—Hoyt Rogers

This selection of Radulescu's poems seems to require translation as a fulfillment of its own project, one that claims the vigor of language as image, a synesthetic trope that appears as early as the first poem with "it's not a word not yet this vapor / escaping my mouth" and elsewhere: "we will taste what is written / on these lips." But the elements of language do not merely populate the poems—enriching if not confusing the readers' senses—their inclusion allows Radulescu to speak to the transience of language, the ways in which denotation dissolves, and each speaker, and perhaps reader, moves into words, the hard rigid shells we inhabit with meaning.

—Emilia Phillips, *Blackbird*

Contents

III. Interviews

Acknowledgments

The following pieces originally appeared (sometimes in earlier versions and under different titles) in the publications indicated:

"The Poem as Devotional Practice: The Lasting Model of the 17th-century English Religious Poets" originally appeared in *Contemporary Poetry Review* and subsequently as the introduction to *Poems of Devotion: An Anthology of Recent Poets* (Wipf & Stock, 2012).

"The Soul's Country: A Review of *Psalms of All My Days*" and "Metaphysical Courage: Bruce Beasley's *Theophobia*" appeared on the *32 Poems* blog.

"Which I is I?: A Review of Books by Scott Cairns, Tarfia Faizullah, and Franz Wright" appeared in *Image* (#83).

"Masterful Variations: A Review of Ashley Anna McHugh's *Into These Knots*" appeared in *Contemporary Poetry Review*.

"Writing From a Life: A Review of Carl Phillips' *Riding Westward*" and "Ignorance and Awe: A Review of Stephen Haven's *Dust and Bread*" appeared in *Indiana Review* (vols. 30.1 and 31.1).

"A Kind of Grace: A Review of Morri Creech's *Field Knowledge*" appeared in *Lyric Poetry Review* (vol. 3.1).

"The Poet and the Priest: A Review of Spencer Reece's *The Road to Emmaus*" appeared on the *Books & Culture* website.

"A Second Experience: A Review of Two Books by Stella Vinitchi Radulescu" appeared in *Asheville Poetry Review* (issue 19, vol. 16.1).

"The *Paris Review* Poetry Purge" appeared in *The Writer's Chronicle* (Oct./Nov. 2010).

"On Virtuosity and Simplicity" and "The Age of Irony" appeared on the *Best American Poetry* blog.

"Magnanimous Despair" and the poem "Weak Devotions" appeared on the blog of the American Public Media radio program "On Being"; "Weak Devotions" originally appeared in *Poetry East* (#69) and subsequently in *Weak Devotions* (Wipf & Stock, 2011) by Luke Hankins.

"The Way They Loved Each Other" (commentary and poem) was broadcast on air on, and also appeared on the blog of, the American Public Media radio program "On Being."

"An Interview at *American Literary Review*" appeared on the *American Literary Review* blog.

"An Interview at *Connotation Press: An Online Artifact*" and the included translations of poems by Stella Vinitchi Radulescu appeared in *Connotation Press: An Online Artifact* (issue IX, vol. V).

There was a subtle flood of steam
Moving upon the face of things.
It came from standing pools and springs
And what of snow was still around;
It came of winter's giving ground
So that the freeze was coming out,
As when a set mind, blessed by doubt,
Relaxes into mother-wit.
Flowers, I said, will come of it.

–Richard Wilbur, from "April 5, 1974"

I. Criticism

The Poem as Devotional Practice

The Lasting Model of the 17th-century
English Religious Poets

I. A Lasting Model?

Certain religious poets of 17th-century England, often called the "Meta-physical" poets, have gained as firm a place in the Western canon as any group of poets enjoys today. Tangibly speaking, that means that they (at least the major four or five) are ubiquitously anthologized, their work remains in print and readily available, there exists a large body of critical work on their poetry and lives, and they are regularly "taught" in post-secondary classrooms, as well as in at least some secondary classrooms. It is clear that they have some measure of significance for scholars, but what influence, if any, do they exert on literature in America today?

II. Defining Devotional Poetry

In reference to 17th-century poets, the term "Metaphysical" has come to indicate certain stylistic tendencies, such as elaborately extended metaphor or conceit, fondness for paradox, and linguistic inventiveness and ingenuity (often loosely termed "wit"). It is strange, considering the etymology of this word and its uses in other contexts, that it should have come to designate stylistic rather than philosophical or spiritual elements. The word was Latinized from Greek in the Middle Ages, and the Latin roots of the word, *meta* and *physic*, might be rendered "over/above" and "nature/the natural," thus indicating the supernatural, the spiritual, or at least the philosophical.[1] In fact, the Greek phrase from which the Latin

---

1. All etymologies discussed in this essay refer to information found in *The Oxford English Dictionary*.

was derived was used as early as the 4th century B.C. as a title for one of Aristotle's treatises, on the subject of ontological philosophy.[2]

However, since Samuel Johnson's largely pejorative remarks about the aims of the "metaphysical" poets, the word has become associated with those stylistic characteristics of the verse that he found offensive or inadequate.[3] We now use the terms "religious" or "devotional" when we want to indicate these poets' spiritual practice and subject matter—though, as I hope to demonstrate, these two terms are not interchangeable, devotional poetry being a specific mode within the larger category of religious poetry.

Anthony Low has done important work in studying 17th-century devotional practice and its relation to the poetry of the time. In his book, *Love's Architecture: Devotional Modes in Seventeenth-Century English Poetry*, he indicates four primary types of devotional practice—vocal, meditative, affective, and contemplative—and demonstrates the ways in which these spiritual exercises influenced the verse of the poets of that age. It often seems implicit in Low's commentary on the poems of the era that the poems are not only informed by or imitative of devotional practice, but are themselves part of that devotional practice, but he does not state this explicitly. Let us state it explicitly, and proceed to support the notion: The composition of a poem may itself be a devotional practice.

We are not likely to be able to know for certain to what extent any given poem was composed as a devotional practice, as opposed to being a re-creation of prior devotional practice or explanation of the outcomes thereof; however, the idea that a poem *can* be a devotional practice is significant and bears being stated and defended. In his essay, "Metaphysical Poets and Devotional Poets," Low says that "Metaphysical poetry is essentially private poetry, that is, poetry that examines and focuses on the inner movements of thought and feeling,"[4] but he comes short of saying that a poem itself can be *a way of thinking*. "In its combination of reason, imagination, and feelings," he goes on to say, "meditation is a close cousin of poetry,"[5] and yet he does not acknowledge poetry as *a means of meditating*. The implication of statements of this kind (wittingly or no on Low's part)

2. "Metaphysical," *Oxford English Dictionary*.

3. John Dryden had made remarks that were even more hostile in the previous century, but he did not designate the poets as "metaphysical," though he did speak of Donne "affect[ing] the metaphysics" (*The Metaphysical Poets* 121).

4. Low, "Metaphysical Poets and Devotional Poets," 224.

5. Ibid., 228.

is that poetry is a recorder of other, prior processes. Literary critics tend to speak this way when they are not thinking like writers. If they were to stop for a moment to consider their own processes in composing their essays or books, they might revise the way they speak of poems, for even an essay is not simply the writing down of fully-formed thoughts, but is a way of organizing and exploring and furthering thought, and is revised in light of the discoveries made in the process of writing.

In his essay, "The Shocking Image," A. D. Nutall says, referring to 17th-century handbooks offering instruction in devotional practice, "The handbooks taught that a man [sic] should train his imagination as an athlete trains his body. It is natural that such a system should produce certain champions, gymnasts of the imagination, whose powers should spill over into their poetry."[6] But Nutall misses the mark when he says that the powers of imagination merely "spill over" into poetry. It makes far more sense to understand the composition of poetry as itself an act of imagination—in other words, not only the *result* of imaginative training, but part of the training itself. Low and Nutall have overlooked the possibility that the composition of a poem can itself be an act of devotion, rather than merely chronicling or imitating or being otherwise influenced by devotional practice. In order to understand this, it is vital to realize that poems are not necessarily begun as foregone conclusions, and, in fact, it would be unlikely for such a poem to prove a lasting work of literature.

Robert Frost famously said that a poem "is but a trick poem and no poem at all if the best of it was thought of first and saved for the last," and that "like a piece of ice on a hot stove the poem must ride on its own melting. [. . .] It can never lose its sense of a meaning that once unfolded by surprise as it went."[7] Denise Levertov offers a similar view in her essay "Some Notes on Organic Form":

> [A]s the poet stands open-mouthed in the temple of life, contemplating his [sic] experience, there come to him the first words of the poem: the words which are to be his way in to the poem, if there is to be a poem. [...] If he forces a beginning before this point, it won't work. [...] [T]he poet, from that moment of being let in to the possibility of the poem, must follow through, letting the experience lead him

---

6. Nuttall, 152.
7. Frost, "The Figure a Poem Makes," 985–986.

through the world of the poem, its unique inscape revealing itself
as he goes.[8]

Great poems are—if not invariably, at least most often—an unfolding, not
only for the reader, but for the poet in the process of composing.

George Herbert, more consistently than any other 17th-century poet,
gives the reader the sense that he is struggling through the poem itself, that
the poem is a tool by which he does his thinking. Take this middle section
from "The Search," for instance:

> Where is my God? What hidden place
>   Conceals thee still?
> What covert dare eclipse thy face?
>   Is it thy will?
>
> O let not that of any thing;
>   Let rather brasse,
> Or steel, or mountains be thy ring,
>   And I will passe.
>
> Thy will such an entrenching is,
>   As passeth thought:
> To it all strength, all subtilties
>   Are things of nought.
>
> Thy will such a strange distance is,
>   As that to it,
> East and West touch, the poles do kisse,
>   And parallels meet.
>
> Since then my grief must be as large,
>   As is thy space,
> Thy distance from me; see my charge,
>   Lord, see my case.
>
> O take these barres, these lengths away,
>   Turn, and restore me:
> Be not Almightie, let me say,
>   Against, but for me.[9]

8. Levertov, 68–69.

9. Herbert, 153–154.

Here, Herbert is agonizing (from the Greek word *agon*—"contest," or *agonia*—"struggle") over the possibility that the distance he feels from God is a result not of anything that stands between himself and God, but of the very will of God. In other words, God has chosen to keep Herbert separate from her/him/it. The feeling that this may be the case causes Herbert to cry out to God to use her/his/its sovereign power for him, rather than against him, or else all hope is lost.

This is a deep kind of wrestling with God, and for the reader it occurs in the present moment of the poem—there is no foregone conclusion here. The poem is so successful in articulating the spiritual struggle that we can speculate that Herbert was actually experiencing a sense of separation from God as he composed the poem—it is at least a possibility—so that the spiritual struggle being dramatized is not simply a re-enactment. We cannot know this for certain, but the very fact that the struggle *seems* to be a present concern of the poet as he writes the poem and that the poem *seems* to be the very devotional means through which Herbert engages with his doubt and communicates with God lends power to the poem. It is doubtful (and I think that Frost and Levertov would have shared my doubt) that a poem as effective as this (and Herbert has many) could have been written toward a foreknown conclusion.

It is true that some 17th-century poems seem to have been written toward a conclusion that was realized before the poem began. This sort of poem might more justly be characterized as a record or imitation of prior spiritual devotion (meditation on a theological mystery, for instance), rather than an act of devotion itself. Some of Donne's "Holy Sonnets" are good examples of this kind of poem. The conclusion of "Holy Sonnet X," for instance, is inherent in first statement of poem. The poem begins with the imperative, "Death be not proud," an order that could not possibly be given by the speaker apart from an already-existing realization of the concluding theological paradox of the poem: "death, thou shalt die."[10] However, it is my contention that many 17th-century poems are examples of exploratory poems—begun in uncertainty of mind and spirit, and themselves representing the devotional process (or at least part of it) through which resolution, or clarity, or simply articulation was achieved.

Although it is, of course, impossible to know, based on the text of the poem alone, to what extent a poet did or did not have the conclusion of the poem in view during the act of composition, we can say this much, at least:

10. Donne, 262.

Some religious poems (like Herbert's "The Search") dramatize a mental or spiritual struggle; other religious poems (like Donne's "Holy Sonnet X") do not purport to dramatize a current struggle, and instead explain or explicate a struggle that happened prior to the composition of the poem. In the latter case, the entire poem functions as a conclusion; even if there is some dramatization, as there is in Donne's poem (a speaker personifying and addressing death), there is no uncertainty in the rhetoric since the conclusion is foreknown and stated or implied from the beginning. This kind of poem engages the reader the way a sermon or an essay might. On the other hand, the rhetoric of a poem that dramatizes a struggle in the literary "present," as Herbert's poem does, proceeds with uncertainty and thus engages the reader the way a play might. This effect is intensified to the extent that the reader senses that the poet's *composition* of the poem proceeded in uncertainty—not only of the literary or formal outcome of the nascent poem, but also the spiritual outcome of engaging the poem's idea.

Perhaps we should now venture a definition of a devotional poem. In order to do so, we should first define devotional practice. For specifics about 17th-century devotional practice, I refer the reader to Anthony Low's book, *Love's Architecture: Devotional Modes in Seventeenth-century English Poetry*. For our purposes, it will suffice to define devotional practice as any of those practices that an individual uses to relate to the divine. Though 17th-century English poets are of particular interest in this essay, devotional practices are not, of course, limited to 17th-century Europeans; they include all intentional ways of relating to the divine in any culture and at any time. I would suggest the following general categories of devotional practice, which are not specific to time period: confession, petition, praise, and meditation (not only in the sense of quieting one's mind, but also in the opposite sense of mental engagement with theological concepts or mysteries, thus including struggle with uncertainty and doubt).

Having defined devotional practice in very broad terms, we can attempt a definition of a devotional poem: A devotional poem represents the devotional practice of the poet (even if it adopts a persona to do so), and is either a re-enactment of the devotional practice or is itself (in the process of its composition) part of that practice. Furthermore, theoretically speaking, a poem whose composition was itself part of the devotional practice would be the quintessential devotional poem, and a poem that re-enacts devotional practice, while remaining in the devotional mode, would fall on the periphery of the category. Thus, the devotional mode can usefully be thought of as a spectrum.

III. Devotional Poetry Today

The Metaphysical poets have exerted a particularly strong influence on American poetry, thus they are the focus of this essay, but so have (and perhaps increasingly so) mystic or ecstatic poets, including Eastern poets such as Rabi'a, Rumi, and Hafiz, as well as Europeans like St. John of the Cross. In fact, we would be remiss to avoid recognizing the mystical or ecstatic poem in any discussion of devotional poetry. The mystical or ecstatic poem can be seen as a sub-category of the devotional poem. However, I would suggest that mystical or ecstatic poems are rarely written by American poets today, and it is primarily in the area of stylistics (rather than mode of composition) that the influence of these poets is evident in contemporary American poetry. On the other hand, it is my contention that a significant number of American poets today still write in the broader devotional mode, and that the primary influence on their practice has been 17th-century English poets—an influence that has less to do with stylistics than with the ways in which their devotional poems engage with uncertainty.

The influence of 17th-century English religious poets transcends stylistics. As Metaphysical poets (if we understand the term to refer to *stylistic* elements), they are inhabitants of a particular time and place; as devotional poets, they inhabit human history, past and future. There are probably no Metaphysical poets today—I certainly know of none—but there are devotional poets. Some poets today occasionally write a poem with a figure that might be considered a metaphysical conceit, for instance, or deal linguistically with paradox in a way that resembles the way the Metaphysicals did, but the stylistic devices of the Metaphysicals are not a lifework for any of our poets. (However, they could be, if anyone were up to the task and inclined toward it—and perhaps, at some point, they *should* be, for the sake of the riches that the practice of the Metaphysical style can make available.) For some, however, poetry is still composed as a devotional practice.

Anthony Low says, "True religious poetry is the product of radical transformation."[11] This gets at what T. S. Eliot identified as the fundamental and vital element in George Herbert's poetry—authenticity:

---

11. Low, *Love's Architecture*, 237.

> When I claim a place for Herbert among those poets whose work every lover of English poetry should read and every student of English poetry should study, irrespective of religious belief or unbelief, I am not thinking primarily of the exquisite craftmanship, the extraordinary metrical virtuosity, or the verbal felicities, but of the *content* of the poems which make up *The Temple*. These poems form a record of spiritual struggle which should touch the feeling, and enlarge the understanding of those readers also who hold no religious belief and find themselves unmoved by religious emotion. (italics Eliot's)[12]

If there could be only one criterion for devotional poetry, it would be authenticity of personal religious or spiritual expression. A devotional poem cannot co-opt religion for non-religious, non-devotional purposes—the poem cannot be ironic in this sense. A devotional poem must be a genuine religious or spiritual expression or practice, otherwise it will simply be a commentary from the outside. Devotional poetry operates from the inside. Furthermore, a devotional poet does not write out of mere nostalgia for childhood religion or out of the influence of scriptural and ecclesiastical language, pure and simple. Rather, a devotional poet engages actively in the pursuit of the divine. Such a poet is literally *devoted* (the etymology indicates "set apart by a vow") to the divine, or its possibility.

A further distinction is necessary, because a devout poet does not necessarily write devotional poetry. Devotional poetry is a distinct category or mode within the larger categories of "religious" and "spiritual" poetry. As I have mentioned in the first section, devotional poetry represents the devotional practice of the poet. A poem may have God, religion, or spirituality as its subject without representing the poet's devotional practice, so that there are religious and spiritual poets who are not devotional poets. W. H. Auden is an excellent example; he is clearly a religious poet, but very rarely a devotional one. Devotional poetry is itself a means of relating with God, rather than simply being a place where theological ideas are explored, and I think Auden's poetry is the latter. For instance, his long poem *For the Time Being: A Christmas Oratorio*, like many of his long poems, is presented from a rhetorical distance, complete with chorus and narrator, so that even though the subject matter is unerringly religious and the ideas clearly theological, they are presented with such formal rhetoric as to make them impersonal.

12. Eliot, 239.

Many of Auden's poems also operate with a tonal irony that is simultaneously humorous and grave—a marvelous effect, of which he is the master—and that makes the poems feel less personal than a devotional poem would. Consider the concluding stanzas of "The More Loving One":

> Admirer as I think I am
> Of stars that do not give a damn,
> I cannot, now I see them, say
> I missed one terribly all day.
>
> Were all stars to disappear or die,
> I should learn to look at an empty sky
> And feel its total dark sublime,
> Though this might take me a little time.[13]

The rhyming couplets in tetrameter lend a "light" quality to this poem, and combined with phrases like "stars that do not give a damn," a humorous effect is achieved. However, the imagined scenario is apocalyptic—the disappearance of all stars from the sky. Just as the scenario is understated, so accordingly is the speaker's response: "I should learn to look at an empty sky / And feel its total dark sublime, / Though this might take me a little time." The confession in the final line strikes the reader as an immense understatement. This kind of irony (in this instance, distance between the tone of the poem and the mood of the speaker, and distance between the statement and its intended meaning) is masterfully wielded in Auden's hand, to great effect. But we can also see how this kind of irony is not suited to the devotional mode, as irony depends for its effect on the "betrayal" of authenticity.

There are some few exceptions in Auden's body of work to the kind of rhetorical and tonal distance noted above—for instance, the poems "The Prophets" and "The Dark Years," which operate without irony and might indeed be considered devotional poems. However, Auden's poetic output from all periods of his life so hinges on irony for its effects that I have chosen not to include his work in this anthology.[14]

Czeslaw Milosz is a fine example of a poet who is usually a religious poet rather than a devotional one, but who has also written some wonderful devotional poems. We do not see the same kind of irony at work in

---

13. Auden, 584.

14. This essay served as an introduction to *Poems of Devotion: An Anthology of Recent Poets* (Wipf & Stock, 2012).

his poems as in Auden's. "An Alcoholic Enters the Gates of Heaven," for instance, from his collection *This,* is addressed directly to God, and it is easy to imagine that the persona of the poem authentically represents the poet himself:

> I pray to you, for I do not know how not to pray.
>
> Because my heart desires you,
> Though I do not believe you would cure me.
>
> And so it must be, that those who suffer will continue to suffer,
> Praising your name.[15]

Uncertainty seems inherent in the above address to God, though it may seem for the reader one step removed from the poet's own uncertainty due to the fact that a persona (an alcoholic) is speaking. "Prayer," however, from the same collection, seems even more clearly in the poet's own voice:

> Now You are closing down my five senses, slowly,
> And I am an old man lying in darkness.
>
> [. . .]
>
> Liberate me from guilt, real and imagined.
> Give me certainty that I toiled for Your glory.
>
> In the hour of the agony of my death, help me with
>   Your suffering
> Which cannot save the world from pain.[16]

The poet (writing this, I believe, in his eighties) is here describing his ongoing encounter with real uncertainty, and we might speculate that the poem was *composed* in uncertainty as well, which situates it more fully in the devotional mode. Often, however, even when we seem to hear Milosz's own voice, it is primarily an appeal to his fellow humans rather than directly to God, as in "If There Is No God," from the last collection published before his death:

> If there is no God,
> Not everything is permitted to man.
> He is still his brother's keeper

15. Milosz, *New & Collected Poems,* 734–735.
16. Ibid., 742–743.

And he is not permitted to sadden his brother,
By saying that there is no God.[17]

Much of Milosz's poetry throughout his life was focused on social, historical, and theological issues, almost always religious to one degree or another,
but less often devotional.

One of the best examples of a contemporary devotional poet writing in America is Franz Wright. There is a host of recent and living poets
who speak about God sporadically or in vague terms, but Franz Wright's
persistence in addressing God directly and specifically in his poems is rare,
certainly among poets honored by the establishment.[18]

In "Letter," from his collection *Walking to Martha's Vineyard*, Wright
writes (in the present tense, you will notice) about a recent religious experience in a church, and then continues the meditation as he recalls walking
outside, remarkably changed in attitude:

> When I step outside the ugliness is so shattering
> it has become dear to me, like a retarded
> child, precious to me.
> If only I could tell someone.
> The humiliation I go through
> when I think of my past
> can only be described as grace.
> We are created by being destroyed.[19]

Wright often deals with guilt arising from his long struggle with depression
and drug and alcohol abuse, as he does here. In this poem, his experience
of guilt has finally been understood as the work of God's grace, and it seems
likely that the composition of the poem was itself part of the process of
coming to that understanding. Wright is drawn to this kind of paradox,
in which something seemingly antagonistic to his faith actually becomes
the instrument through which he experiences God, time and again in his
meditations. In "Cloudless Snowfall," he says, "thank You for / keeping Your
face hidden, I / can hardly bear the beauty of this world."[20] In "Year One,"
he writes, "Moonlit winter clouds the color of the desperation of wolves. //

---

17. Milosz, *Second Space*, 5.
18. Wright was awarded the Pulitzer Prize in 2004.
19. Wright, *Walking to Martha's Vineyard*, 38–39.
20. Ibid., 24.

Proof / of Your existence? There is nothing / but."[21] Wright addresses this paradox in an interview with Ernest Hilbert:

> I think what [George] Herbert is getting at ([Gerard Manley] Hopkins is marvelous at this, too) is that our suffering is the terrible and only teacher—Kierkegaard said famously suffering is the characteristic of God's love—and I think everyone senses that failure and brokenness and loneliness cause us to perceive us as God might, as naked and ignorant and blind. Our suffering may be the real form love takes, but we also know that at the end of it waits infinite peace and radiance, that has been my experience anyway. Why things are arranged this way, who knows—pretty soon we are all going to find out.[22]

Wright believes in the grace of God being mediated through suffering to such an extent that he is able to write, "Fill me with love for the *truly* afflicted / that hopeless love, if need be / make me one of them again."[23] And similarly, in "The Process," he writes about his experience of unpredictable and inexplicable joy, as well as its inverse—unpredictable and inexplicable agony. The movement of the poem is into an attitude of submission to and acceptance of God's will, even if it requires his relapse into "the long black killing years" that "can always come again // according to Your will." He concludes, "this time / I will not whine, I will obey // and be / (forever) / still."[24]

In his interview with Hilbert, Wright seems to indicate that the composition of his poems is very much a devotional process. He says, "I would say that the one and only reward of writing is the experience of writing—if you take it seriously, technically and spiritually—the experience, that secret glory, itself."[25] And in another interview, with Ilya Kaminsky and Katherine Towler, he says, "Writing is listening. Religious experience is silent listening and waiting. I have always been able to tell whether something I am writing is genuinely an expression of revelation or if it's just me exercising my intellect. I can feel the difference, see it and taste it, but I don't know how I can do that."[26] In "Kyrie," a poem from Wright's collection *Wheeling Motel*,

21. Ibid., 3.
22. Hilbert, "The Secret Glory."
23. Wright, "Why is the Winter Light," *God's Silence*, 90–91.
24. Ibid., 135.
25. Hilbert, "The Secret Glory."
26. Kaminsky and Towler, "A Conversation with Franz Wright."

he writes, "he was legibly told what to say and he wrote // with mounting excitement and pleasure . . . ."[27] The "he" of this poem is certainly the poet, discovering what it is he will write as he writes it—as it is dictated to him from outside.

In Wright's poem "The Only Animal," he writes,

> this morning
> I stood once again
> in this world, the garden
> ark and vacant
> tomb of what
> I can't imagine,
> between twin eternities,
> some sort of wings,
> more or less equidistantly
> exiled from both,
> hovering in the dreaming called
> being awake, where
> You gave me
> in secret one thing
> to perceive, the
> tall blue starry
> strangeness of being
> here at all.[28]

The "strangeness of being" is an enduring uncertainty about which the poet meditates, presumably both in moments like the one described in the poem and through the very composition of this and other poems.

In Wright's poetry, uncertainty is often the impetus for the writing, and the writing is a means of engaging the uncertainty in an act of devotion (a meditation, often explicitly addressed to God). These are the poems of Wright's that are most fully devotional. He does, however, have many poems that seem to record devotional experiences rather than enact them in their composition; these poems remain in the devotional mode, though more peripherally than poems like "The Only Animal." But in general, Wright's poetry is devotional in the truest sense of the word—not only does it record religious experience and devotional practice, but it is often itself part of that devotional practice, which for Wright involves "listening" and "revelation."

27. Wright, *Wheeling Motel*, 7.

28. Wright, *Walking to Martha's Vineyard*, 73–75.

But Wright is not alone. The 77 poets in this anthology[29] demonstrate that the devotional mode is not a relic of a particular time period or cultural paradigm, but is rather a vital, living artistic mode. I chose to include poets who were alive in 1950 and afterward for this very purpose. From now-canonical voices like T. S. Eliot and Theodore Roethke which resound with authority, to the deep interiority of poets like Patrice de la Tour du Pin and R. S. Thomas; from the monastic perspectives of Madeline DeFrees and Thomas Merton, to worldly-wise voices like Denise Levertov and Mary Karr; from the thoughtful songwriters Leonard Cohen and Sufjan Stevens, to the dramatic monologues of Andrew Hudgins, Maurice Manning, and Ashley Anna McHugh; from Amit Majmudar's mystical Islamic setting of *Paradise Lost*, to Bruce Beasley's fragmented and searching self-portrait; from Jane Hirshfield's intuition of an otherness, to the Orthodox meditations of Scott Cairns; from well-known figures like Charles Wright, Louise Glück, Agha Shahid Ali, and Mark Jarman, to lesser-known, extraordinary poets like Judy Little, Stella Vinitchi Radulescu, Philip Metres, and Malachi Black; from 1888 to 1991—these poets testify to the ongoing importance of the devotional mode in poetry.

These poets are not Metaphysical poets, but they are devotional ones in the long tradition of the Old Testament psalmists, medieval mystical poets, 17th-century English poets, and later devotional poets like Gerard Manley Hopkins and Rainer Maria Rilke. Together, the poets included in this anthology demonstrate that stylistics are constantly changing in poetry, but devotion itself endures, with the power to, in Eliot's phrase, "touch the feeling, and enlarge the understanding."[30]

29. That is, *Poems of Devotion: An Anthology of Recent Poets* (Wipf & Stock, 2012).
30. Eliot, 239.

Which I is I?

A Review of Three Poetry Collections

Idiot Psalms by Scott Cairns (Paraclete Press, 2014)

Seam by Tarfia Faizullah (Southern Illinois University Press, 2013)

F by Franz Wright (Alfred A. Knopf, 2013)

In the long history of the poetry of religious devotion, one often encounters a guileless representation of the self in its attempts to relate to the divine. The speaker of an Old Testament psalm, for instance, will speak directly to God without tonal or narrative irony, presumably in a voice that accurately represents the writer's own thoughts and feelings; the speaker of a mystical poem by Rumi or Rabi'a al Basri will address the beloved divine with the same directness and simplicity of expression the poet would use in private prayer. But with the rise of Modernism, Existentialism, and Postmodernism, as religious faith was called increasingly and more broadly into question, so was the concept of the self. Intellectuals of the 20th century grew more dubious about such inherited notions as the consistency and uniformity of the self, as well as the ability to legitimately represent the self in art. We see in the work of Gerard Manley Hopkins—a priest and poet living, as it were, between Romanticism and Modernism—one of the most significant manifestations of Western culture's evolving concept of the self. In what are known as his "Terrible Sonnets," for instance, the self that relates to God and the self that speaks in a poem are indeed intended to be one and the same, and yet the florid and elaborate language indicates an attempt to express the complexities of the individual spiritual experience in novel ways. Hopkins, more than any other poet since the 17th century, experimented with sounds and rhythms in a way that infused new expressive possibilities into language as an artistic medium, and thus pioneered new ways of examining the self in its relation not only to language, but also—through language—to God.

Later, in the full flush of Modernism, Theodore Roethke wrote, "My soul, like some heat-maddened summer fly / Keeps buzzing at the sill. Which I is I?"[1] In response to such concerns, artists of the 20th century explored new modes of expression in order to do some justice to the ambiguity of the self. From Surrealism with its wild juxtapositions and dislocations, to stream-of-consciousness writing; from the linguistic experiments and games of the French writers' group Oulipo, to Cubism's radical reimagining of perception and perspective; from Minimalism's almost-silence, to the postmodern tendency toward ironic expression, these and a host of other approaches to making art arose, in part, in an attempt to explore novel notions of the self. But most of the artists thus engaged were decidedly secular, paying little or no attention to the relation of the self, in all of its complexity, to God, in all of God's complexity. (There are, of course, notable exceptions: Marianne Moore, T. S. Eliot, Denise Levertov, John Berryman, Mark Rothko, and Arvo Pärt, to name a few). Nevertheless, the ideas and concerns raised primarily by secular movements have been deeply relevant to spiritual art and literature, and engagement with them has been one of the most important developments of 20th- and 21st-century spiritual literature. The books currently under review demonstrate this ongoing engagement, presenting the reader with challenging representations of the self in relation to the divine.

~

Scott Cairns is the author of a large body of exceptionally incisive poetry and prose on spiritual matters. As a participant in the Greek Orthodox tradition, his work often delves into the nuances of the biblical and theological uses of the Greek language. In his latest collection of poems, *Idiot Psalms*, Cairns also offers some poems based on his numerous pilgrimages to Mount Athos in Greece to spend time in prayer and meditation among the monks who reside there. This autobiographical element is balanced with a series of "Idiot Psalms," each identified in a headnote as "a psalm of Isaak." The persona Cairns has created is presumably named after the Old Testament patriarch, and possibly also the 7th-century Saint Isaak of Syria, a major figure in the Greek Orthodox tradition. However, the strange and often humorous use of archaic language mixed with the spiritual concerns

---

1. Roethke, 231.

of a modern believer's daily life gives the reader a clue that the persona of Isaak is a fictionalized version of the poet himself. Through Isaak, Cairns gives voice to spiritual dilemmas that undoubtedly characterize Cairns' own life, and yet the voice is certainly not Cairns' everyday one:

> Why, O Blithely *Un*apparent, do you remain
>   serenely imperceptible, even to our thinning
>   crew who stand here blinking at the sky?
> I have no stomach for the newspapers, no heart
>   for the brilliant, lit flat-screen catalog
>   of woes, though every item flickers,
>   one admits, wondrously produced
>   and duly sponsored.[2]

The characterization of this persona as an "idiot"—or at least the producer of "idiot psalms"—is clarified by some of the epigraphs included in various sections of the book: for instance, Cairns quotes Prince Myshkin from Dostoevsky's *The Idiot*, who says that "one must first begin by not understanding many things!" In another section, he cites Saint Paul's epistle to the Colossians: "Let him become a fool, that he may be wise." And so the kind of idiocy in which Cairns is interested in these poems is that of a holy fool, one with the kind of childlike faith that Jesus celebrates in the Gospels:

> Make me to awaken daily with a willingness
>   to roll out readily, accompanied
>   by grateful smirk, a giddy joy,
>   the idiot's undying expectation,
>   despite the evidence.[3]

At times Isaak seems a stand-in for the poet himself; at others, he seems an everyman figure; at others yet, he seems more closely related to his biblical namesake, as in "Idiot Psalm 1," where he describes himself as being "shy / of immolation," a hint at Isaak's childhood experience as the object of a divinely initiated, and divinely aborted, sacrifice by his father, Abraham:

> Once more, O Lord, from Your Enormity incline
>   your Face to shine upon Your servant, shy
>   of immolation, if You will.[4]

---

2. Cairns, "Idiot Psalm 6," 39.

3. Ibid., "Idiot Psalm 2," 21.

4. Ibid., 13.

The biblical Isaak's primal experience of the divine as one of terror and violence can be seen as a metaphor for the ways in which our earliest spiritual experiences shape the way we relate to God throughout our lives. In the above psalm, Isaak is "fool" enough to overcome fear in order to request God's presence once again. In Isaak, Cairns combines aspects of historical religious figures, invented character, and the poet's own identity in order to illuminate the experience of prayer. Isaak's multifaceted, shapeshifting nature is a fascinating illustration of the complexity of the self in its spiritual labor.

Outside the Isaak poems, we often see the poet expressly searching for a means of rendering his experience, and always finding both metaphor and language insufficient:

To What Might This Be Compared?

As one peering, fixed,
    into the icon's
        limpid eye observes
a subtle quickening,
    just there, beyond
        the opaque plane—

As one tugging up
    his socks and lacing
        sturdy boots to take
another season's
    turn around the Holy
        Mountain's desert span—

As one, crushed again
    by failed, flailing prayer
        finds of a moment
and in the stillness
    of the cave a breath
        both cool and welcoming—

so I observed yet
    one more chance reprieve,
        shook my head, and rose.[5]

---

5. Ibid., 41.

Here, the reader never even discovers what exactly the subject of all the attempted metaphors—that "chance reprieve" (merely a locution for the subject)—is. In this way, the act of making metaphor itself—that attempt to make meaning from experience—becomes the real subject of the poem. Likewise, in "Heavenly City (*Ouranoúpoli*)," Cairns writes, alluding to his time on Mount Athos,

> [. . .] The world remains a puzzle,
>
> no matter how many weeks one stands
> apart from it, no matter how one tries
>
> to see its troubled surfaces, or hopes
> to dip beneath them for a glimpse of what it is
>
> that makes this all appear to tremble so.[6]

Despite the apparent insufficiency of our perception of the world, and the insufficiency of metaphor and language, here we have Cairns' poems—an implicit argument that the failed attempt itself is expressive of our nature and our experience. Would there be anything truly human, truly indicative of the self, Cairns seems to be asking us, in a metaphor that was fully satisfactory, in a description that did full justice to its subject? Art, like "failed, flailing prayer," is valuable despite—no, *because of* its insufficiency:

> [. . .] Sure, I'm making this up as I go, hoping—even
> as I go—to be finally getting somewhere.
> And maybe I am.
>
> Maybe I'm taking you along. Let's say it's so, and say
> however late the hour we now commence.[7]

Come, reader—join Cairns on the fool's errand of his *Idiot Psalms*.

~

Tarfia Faizullah is a talented young poet whose first collection, *Seam*, received the Crab Orchard Series in Poetry First Book Award. This collection arose from Faizullah's interviews, supported by a Fullbright fellowship, with women who were victims of rape and abuse during the 1971 War of

---

6. Ibid., 56–57.
7. Ibid., "Speculation Along the Way," 52.

Independence between Pakistan and what is now Bangladesh. Faizullah's work shuttles back and forth over time and place, weaving together Texas and Bangladesh, her mother's past and the poet's own life:

> In west Texas, oil froths
> luxurious from hard ground
> while across Bangladesh
>
> bayoneted women stain
> pond water blossom. Your
> mother, age eight, follows
>
> your grandmother down worn
> stone steps to the old pond . . . .[8]

Faizullah opens her collection with a number of poems that examine her own position as someone a generation removed from Bangladesh, and yet part of the living history of her family, as she takes upon herself the project of traveling from her home in America to investigate the histories of women in Bangladesh. This is the first element that complicates the self in *Seam*—Faizullah's attempt to integrate her identity geographically and genealogically. The middle portion of the book is composed of a series of poems in which the speaker interviews *birangonas*—"war heroines" from the Bangladeshi War of Independence, so called retrospectively in an attempt to honor them because of the abuse they suffered—with notes and asides interspersed. Living in Bangladesh, hearing these women's stories, and considering her own position as someone observing the suffering from the outside leads the speaker to moments of psychological and spiritual crisis—the second element that complicates the self in these poems.

In "Reading Willa Cather in Bangladesh," Faizullah writes:

> Each day, I begin
>
> to disappear into yards
>
> of silk or cotton—
>
> the one that is me but not
>
> begins to emerge,

---

8. Faizullah, "1971," 1.

coaxed out by each hand

pressed against me,

   its desire to remember—

cousin, aunt, beggar,

   vendor . . . .⁹

Here, the self is disconcerted by a seemingly novel aspect of the self that "begins to emerge," as if it were a separate being. The speaker recognizes it as "one that is me but not." This crisis of identity intensifies, the more she delves into the stories of the *birangonas*, one of whom is the speaker of these lines:

[. . .] Don't you know

they made us watch her head fall
from the rusted blade of the old

jute machine? That they made us
made us made us made us made us?¹⁰

Through repetition, the meaning of "made us" at the end of this poem morphs from "forced us to" into "shaped us" or "formed us." The tragic truth Faizullah encounters is that God is not the only maker, but we are made, over and over, by others' actions and by our experiences. It is fitting that the speaker herself is undergoing an intense period of being remade as she faces this reality in the stories related by the *birangonas*.

In "The Interviewer Acknowledges Shame," the speaker returns to her hotel room after interviewing, lies down on the bed, and masturbates. The shame referred to in the title is not, as one might anticipate, the shame of experiencing physical pleasure while on a mission to understand the suffering of others, but rather:

[. . .] It's when she sits down naked
   at the desk to rewind and fast-forward through

9. Ibid., 35.
10. Ibid., "Interview with a Birangona," 30–31.

all the pixelated footage of the women's
    kerosene lives. It's when
she begins to write about it in third person,
    as though it was that simple
to unnail myself from my own body.[11]

When the speaker fully inhabits her own body, with its pain and its pleasure, she feels no shame. It is only when she undertakes the project of writing about her interviews with the *birangonas*, and in so doing attempts to
achieve a degree of remove from her own visceral reactions in a journalistic
impulse toward objectivity, that she feels ashamed. As becomes clear in the
final lines of this poem, such objectivity is not possible for the speaker. For
Faizullah, maintaining the façade would be dishonest; thus she abruptly
switches from third person to first in the final line, jarring the reader not
only with the violence of the image—"unnail myself from my own body"—
but also with the sudden intimacy of the speaker's unveiling of herself.

The vicissitudes of the speaker's evolving sense of self bear on her relation to the divine. Early in the collection, she senses a divide not only geographically and generationally, but also between her desire to offer spiritual
comfort and her sense that such an attempt might be empty:

Two weeks ago I crossed two oceans wide as
the funeral processions to your grave:

bearded men continued to thumb plastic
prayer beads beside your sheet-swaddled

body. Grandmother, in Virginia, I cradled
the phone to my cheek and stood over the dark

skillet, waiting to turn over another slice
of bacon to slip into my mouth, knowing

well that sin, too, like so many others,
would dissolve once I willed it to. *Allah-er borosha,*

I mumbled to your daughter: *It's Allah's will:*
words I knew couldn't fill even that half-filled

suitcase spilled out across hardwood floor . . . .[12]

11. Ibid., 43.

12. Ibid., "Elegy with Her Red-tipped Fingers," 17.

Later, at an Independence Day celebration in Dakha, the speaker addresses and questions God, interspersing lines from Paul Celan's work as a way of giving voice to her dilemmas:

> In a courtyard, in these stacks of chairs
> before the empty stage—*near are*
> *we Lord, near and graspable.* Lord,
> accept these humble offerings:
>
> stacks of biscuits wrapped in cellophane,
> stacks of bone in glass: thighbone,
> spine. Stacks of white saucers, porcelain
> circles into which stacks of lip-worn
>
> cups slide neat. Jawbone, Lord. Galleries
> of laminated clippings declaring war.
> Hands unstack chairs into rows. *The dead:*
> *they still go begging.* What for, Lord?
>
> Blunt bayonets, once sharp as wind?
> Moon-pale stacks of clavicle? A hand—[13]

Faizullah does not receive answers to her questions, nor does she experience an epiphany that reveals her essential identity to herself in a conclusive way. She knows better than to reach for such facile, dishonest ways of writing about inner turmoil. Just as she has the honesty to admit to herself the façade of the third-person objective voice in her own poems, Faizullah has the integrity to leave the dilemmas of her self, her family homeland's history, and her relationship with God unresolved, presented to the reader in all their messy humanness.

~

It might justly be said that the self is the central subject of the entire tradition of lyric poetry. And yet, some poets remain closer to the thinking and feeling center of the human than others, rather than looking consistently outward as observer, and more often regard the self itself than exterior phenomena. Few remain closer to that center than Franz Wright. His detractors would certainly single out this involution. And yes, it is true that Wright has long epitomized the Woe Is Me school of poetry. There is ubiquitous evidence of this in his body of work, but as the book currently under

13. Ibid., "Reading Celan at the Liberation War Museum," 51.

consideration also contains plentiful evidence there is no need to consult the archives. Consider, for instance, even the title of his latest book: *F*, his initial, which he addresses in the long prose poem at the center of this collection, "Entries of the Cell":

> And look what I've come across in the middle of these disintegrating pages.
> It's a capital *F* that takes up a whole page.
>
> My name, or grade in life?
>
> In color a dull dead rust-red, someone's blood, and I can't imagine whose.[14]

Consider also the epigraph to the book:

> The Hacs have arranged to rear every year a few child martyrs . . . raggedy, wretched, hopeless kids . . . whom they subject to atrocious mistreatment and evident injustices, inventing reasons and deceptive complications based on lies, for everything, in an atmosphere of terror and mystery. In this way they have brought up great artists, poets. (Henri Michaux)[15]

Wright's greatest flaw as a writer is his hyper-Romantic notion of the poet as—to use Michaux's term—martyr. The reader often gets the sense that Wright sees himself as a *poète maudit*, wandering the blasted heath alone, suffering depths of torment unfathomed by any but fellow poets. This view of what it means to be a poet is flawed—as if there were emotional, psychological, or circumstantial criteria that made one writer a "poet" and another simply a writer of verse. To title his latest book with his own initial, and to imply via the epigraph from Michaux that poets are burdened with a particularly onerous allocation of suffering is not worthy of Wright's better moments, in which his consideration moves outward from personal anguish to empathy for others, particularly children:

> Right at the moment I am sitting at a very small desk beside a small child who can't write, doesn't draw or play much, and has never said a single word to anyone as far as I know.
>
> A flawlessly beautiful child with perfect white sharp tiny teeth, long straight blonde hair, and profoundly intelligent dark blue

14. Wright, *F*, 40.
15. Ibid., vii.

sad eyes. A perfectly lovely little girl who has no name, and is one hundred thousand years old.[16]

We also see here a touch of the Surrealist influence on Wright's work, in which youth and age are perceived simultaneously in the child, and in which time itself loses its usual hold on our daily experience.

Another admirable quality of Wright's work evident in the above is his defiance of accepted writerly wisdom: the idea that one should avoid adjectives and adverbs as much as possible is so widely advocated that it has become a platitude students hear in any Writing 101 class or textbook. But Wright's deliberate superabundance of adjectives and adverbs in the above stanza contributes to not only the precision of his observation of the child ("perfect white sharp tiny teeth"), but also the mood of rapture, which enables the reader to leap into the surreal with the speaker at the end, where the child is described as "one hundred thousand years old."

While we must admit that Wright's work consistently takes the poet's or the speaker's own suffering as its subject, we often see as well a moving desire to reach others who might be suffering in ways Wright is familiar with. There is compassion and magnanimity at the heart of many of his poems:

> When you have to take it to feel, more
> or less, the way you once felt
> when you weren't taking it,
>
> I'll meet you at high moon.
>
> I'll greet you
> there, the other
> last speaker of a language.
>
> At the trial of sleep,
>
> theoretically, I will be seeing you.
> In the aisles of the pharmacy
> open all night, I'll be waiting. Outside
>
> the locked glass door to the insane
> asylum dollhouse childhoods
> like yours, I'll keep vigil[17]

16. Ibid., "Entries of the Cell," 37.
17. Ibid., "One," 23.

Wright also has a fascinating spiritual understanding of the importance of suffering for the development of the soul. In an interview with Ernest Hilbert, Wright said, in reference to the 17th-century poet George Herbert:

> I think what Herbert is getting at (Hopkins is marvelous at this, too) is that our suffering is the terrible and only teacher—Kierkegaard said famously suffering is the characteristic of God's love—and I think everyone senses that failure and brokenness and loneliness cause us to perceive us as God might, as naked and ignorant and blind. Our suffering may be the real form love takes, but we also know that at the end of it waits infinite peace and radiance, that has been my experience anyway.[18]

Likewise, in *F* he writes, "Anguish, grieving: you will get over them. That's the problem."[19] And so Wright's greatest flaw—an obsession with and romanticization of the suffering self—is perhaps also the source of his most profound insights.

Although Wright's poems deal with subject matter from his own life—drug dependency, mental disorders, institutionalization, religious epiphany and conversion—it would be a mistake to read the poems as simple or pure autobiography. Wright's concern is always aesthetic; that is, he wants to offer the reader an aesthetic experience that is faithful not so much to the literal events of his life as to his lived experience—the *feeling* of his life. To think of his work as "Confessional" would be to miss the point of it entirely. (Indeed, the term "Confessional" in relation to poetry has in recent years—and rightly so—come under much scrutiny.) And so when we read

> But I've said all that
> I had to say.
> In writing.
> I signed my name.
> It's death's move.[20]

—which seems to allude to Wright's doubt about whether he would continue to write, publicly stated during his recent bout with lung cancer—we note first of all that the poem appears on page 25 of this book, and that there is plenty of writing that follows. But the reader can certainly identify

18. Hilbert, "The Secret Glory."
19. Wright, *F*, "Entries of the Cell," 40.
20. Ibid., "Crumpled-up Note Blowing Away," 25.

with the speaker's sense of futility and resignation, and clearly for Wright that is the point.

The self presented in Wright's poems is characterized by a complex mixture of morbid and self-derogatory humor, anger, sarcasm, childlike simplicity, and ecstatic bursts of lyricism, as in "Dedication":

> [. . .] I cannot
> seem to write
> from this gray institution. See
> we are so busy trying to cure me;
> and I'm condemned—sorry, I have been given the job
> of vacuuming the desert forever, well, no less than eight hours a
>   day.
> And it's really just about a thousand miles of cafeteria;
> a large one in any event. With its miniature plastic knives,
> its tuna salad and saran-wrapped genitalia will somebody please
> get me out of here, sorry. I am happy to say that
> every method, massive pharmaceuticals, art therapy
> and edifying films as well as others I would prefer
> not to mention—I mean, every single technique
> known to the mouth—sorry!—to our most kindly
> compassionate science is being employed
> to restore me to normal well-being
> and cheerful stability. I go on vacuuming,
> toward a small diamond light burning
> off in the distance.[21]

This self, this character who is the speaker of Wright's poems, is able to consider subjects of great complexity and metaphysical import in a way that immediately disarms and engages the reader. "I am more concerned," he says in "Screamed Lullaby," "to tell you the truth, with the eternity that preceded my birth than its famous counterpart in whose presence I will soon be basking, or so I have been told."[22] The fine-tuned phrases in this sentence—"famous counterpart," "basking," and "or so I have been told"— contribute a mildly humorous sarcasm and a note of doubt that don't detract from the seriousness of his meditation, but invite the reader to relax in its presence.

Although this slightly ironic tone is the dominant mode for Wright, there are moments where it seems that every pretense falls away, and the

21. Ibid., "Dediction," 49.
22. Ibid., 65.

speaker bares his emotion and his mind before God. These moments are all the more powerful for their contrast to the intentionally flimsy shield of irony that most often characterizes Wright's poems:

> For all intents and purposes abandoned, Your love unrequited, You have not turned away from my mind, its former numb and sleepless coma. And I know my failure to perceive You can in no way diminish the fact that You are here![23]

Wright's work embodies our own inability, except in rare moments, to relate without pretense and without intellectual impediment to the divine. One need not share Wright's particular faith or manner of addressing the divine to see one's own spiritual condition illustrated in both his speaker's flaws and his momentary triumphs. And so we can be glad that, as all indications suggest, Wright will continue his poetic vocation.[24]

~

The poem in which Theodore Roethke poses to himself the question "Which I is *I*?" concludes with these lines: "The mind enters itself, and God the mind, / And one is One, free in the tearing wind."[25] And this is precisely what the poets under discussion here do: They delve into the depths of the self ("The mind enters itself"), surfacing not with answers but with powerful expressions of the irresolvable dilemma of selfhood. And it is through this expression of the mystery of the self and its relation to the divine that the reader feels most intimately connected with the searching mind behind the poems, recognizing the quest and the questions as her own. And so "one is One": through art, we are unified one with another—and with the Other.

23. Ibid, "Entries of the Cell," 31.
24. This was written before Wright's death on May 14, 2015.
25. Roethke, 231.

Metaphysical Courage

A Review of Bruce Beasley's *Theophobia*

Theophobia by Bruce Beasley (BOA Editions, 2012)

The title of Beasley's latest book, *Theophobia*, reminds us that Western religious conceptions of God are inextricably bound to the idea and the experience of fear. The God of Judaism and Christianity is a figure worthy of not only respect but also dread. One of Beasley's epigraphs for this book is Proverbs 1:7, "The dread of the Lord is the beginning of wisdom." This "theophobia" and the range of its possible manifestations are at the heart of Beasley's poems and, one must suppose, at the heart of the poet's personal agon with skepticism and belief.

Beasley's poems, not only in this collection but throughout his work, repeatedly raise the moral considerations inherent in the idea of a Creator who is dreadful as well as glorious. One of the most effective ways Beasley engages these considerations is by examining natural phenomena through the lens of scientific learning, notably in the fields of genetics, neuroscience, animal biology, and disease. In earlier books, astrophysics and cosmology also figure largely. Consider, for instance, the following excerpts from "Extremophilic Magnificat," which references the biblical hymn of praise that Mary offers upon being told that she will give birth to the Messiah, and which bears the epigraph "Awe . . . was an awful Mother, but I liked him better than none" (Emily Dickinson). In this poem, Beasley considers two creatures that live in extreme conditions deep in the ocean, the Pompeii worm and the bone-eating snotflower:

from (I) Pompeii Worm

This near-boiling geyser-gush   through the Earth's crust
blasted water
acidic as vinegar
on Galapagos'   seabed, this

papery tube the extremophile
Pompeii worm drills
to make   its habitation in a black-
smoker hydrotherm   rift-zone chimney

[…]

[…] waving   the feathers of a gray

shawl   made wholly
out of symbiotic bacteria
into and out of the magma—

Theo-
phobe,

what can *you*
do
with these creatures, these
living filaments that fur the worm's back and feed
off sugared mucus   it oozes

and repay their host by denitrifying,
sulfur-eating, detoxifying
the sulfide   jets so pressured by   the mile-
deep sea they can't break into boil?

from (II) Bone-eating Snotflower

Lord, Theos, down here they call those   monstrous bodies
    hopeful whose
genetic spasms of deformation
amount to a *saltation*,
a leap   into a wholly new species

Evolution's   random hypervariation

I call it *theurgy*   God-work

[...]

from (III) Annunciation to Mary, and Her Hymn of Praise the Magnificat

Hail, bulged   ovisac and dwarf male
mucofloris,

[...]
the Lord is with thee   too, in involuntary
sanctifying
at the vent-site, and toxin-purifying
eurytheotic
me, [...]

[...]

Our bodies—bacterial-
fuzzed and toxin-eating, scald-

loving, tentacles over a hundred
thousand eggs surrounded
by a swarm of third-
of-a-millimeter
males—do   *magnify the Lord* whether or not we want them
     to ...

[...]

Should we
keep
all these things in the depths   as if we'd never
spoken of them, or call   ourselves hopeful
monsters like these, un-
fathom
all they say   as they wave
pink gill-plumes over
their gray and brain-shaped ovaries?[1]

1. Beasley, 72–76.

Beasley believes that if the natural world is created, it is itself—including our own bodies—the revelation of its Creator. But that's precisely the problem. Is there any coherence in the revelation? Is interpretation possible? And who are we, as part of the system being examined (we "hopeful monsters"), to say what *we* might mean—or indeed who we might be? When we are our own subjects of investigation, surely objectivity is impossible:

> As if the exegesis—of DNA's
> scripture & scat—could ever cease.
>
> As though some ineradicable trait
> translated out of the incoherent
>
> lingua prima of gene could tear
>
> my *self* apart, mitotic, strand by strand—
>
> [...]
>
> Can't we say
> anymore, with Descartes, *the soul*
> *can work independently of the brain,*
> can we say anymore, with Descartes,
> *ignoramus et ingorabimus, we are ignorant*
> *and shall so remain?*
>
> Tell me, snipped thread, warped ladder,
> what it is you say I am.
> Nucleus-cosmographer, hymn me
> the six-billion-lettered song of self.[2]

The self is far too complex, multifaceted, and labile to allow for us to get a coherent sense of who we are, much less of what the metaphysical significance of our nature and existence might be. The continued discoveries of science have made it clearer than ever that the Rationalist hopes of Cartesian philosophy are doomed to failure. What reason has shown us, in fact, is that our reason cannot sound the complexities of such fundamental concepts as "self," disallowing a "first philosophy" of any certainty. And yet, we are faced with a dilemma because we are creatures always inclined to seek answers to the riddle of being—as Beasley says, "As if the exegesis [...] could

2. Ibid., "Genomic Vanitas," 49.

ever cease." Thankfully, however, Beasley does not attempt to provide answers, but rather offers to the reader his experience of the dilemma itself in compelling and surprising ways. What do we seek more fundamentally in art than powerful expression of the human condition? Art does not provide answers. Art convinces us that we are not alone in asking the questions.

If the natural world for Beasley is a language that speaks of God's nature and attributes, it is an often strange and frightening language, and, like art, one which does not provide answers so much as provoke questions. In an extended metaphor of Metaphysical proportions, worthy of John Donne, Beasley writes:

> Being-Without-a-Body, get
> to me
> and shiver along the nerves
>
> like the *Toxoplasma gondii* parasite
> that works its way deep up a rat's brain
> and lays its cysts all through the amygdala,
>
> unsnips the dendrites from networks
> of instinctive fear that repel
> the rat from cat pheromones, and reconnects
>
> the wiring so the rat's testes swell
> with attraction at the smell
> of cat-piss and so urge the rat straight toward
>
> the predator's mouth, since a cat-gut's
> the only place where toxoplasma can breed, and the parasite
>   leaves
> the cat's body in the feces another rat will eat
>
> and that rat's brain will also be restrung
> from dread to lust for what consumes it: Spirit
> of Holy Fear, who's afraid?[3]

God as invading organism. God as death sentence. And yet this is a prayer *to be invaded, to be sentenced to death.* Is this masochism? Suicidal desire? Or is it an accusation against God's goodness?

I think none of these. What we see in Beasley's work is an unflagging observation of things-as-they-are, including terrible aspects of our world

3. Ibid., "Having Read the Holy Spirit's Wikipedia," 12–13.

and our experiences in it. In such a world, to entertain the idea of a Creator is necessarily to call the Creator's motives and character into question. But in face of barbarism in the natural world and personal psychological suffering, Beasley's poems communicate not simple horror or outrage or confusion, but ultimately wonder, awe at the complexity of the systems—both material and psychological—in which suffering occurs.

In the excerpt above from "Having Read the Holy Spirit's Wikipedia," I suggest that it is Beasley's awe that wins out over his horror. It is a prayer—a fearful one, yes ("Spirit / of Holy Fear, who's afraid?")—of surrender of the self to a system that supersedes the self, in which annihilation of the self may contribute to the terrible beauty of the whole.

Does this trouble you, dear reader?

Exactly.

Beasley possesses what I would call metaphysical courage—something great philosophers, theologians, and artists must possess. It is the ability to consider negative possibilities without faltering and without recourse to facile idealized assumptions. It is akin to, but not identical with, Keats' idea of "negative capability." Whereas negative capability avoids any "irritable reaching after fact and reason,"[4] metaphysical courage continually reaches after "fact and reason"—but it refuses to settle for comforting illusions. Beasley's spirituality is not one of false comfort, but rather one that arises out of, and ultimately accepts as crucial, fear itself. He is willing to be troubled if that is what our experience of the world calls for—if that is part of our existential ecosystem.

If, as Beasley asserts, the world and its processes are "God-work" ("Extremophilic Magnificat"), what do they tell us about God? One of the two epigraphs to this book is from Leszek Kołakowski's *Metaphysical Horror*:

> One might ask why, if the universe is indeed a secret book of the gods with a coded message for us, this message is not written in ordinary language rather than in hieroglyphics whose decoding is discouragingly arduous and, above all, never results in certainty. But this question is futile, for two independent reasons. First, it assumes that we do know, or can imagine, what the universe would be like if its message and meaning were clearly readable and unambiguously displayed before our eyes. But we do not know this, and we lack the kind of imagination necessary to imagine it. Second, it is possible that if we knew *why* the message is hidden, or partly hidden, it would no longer be hidden—in other words, that

4. Keats, *The Letters . . .* , 193–194.

concealment of the reasons for which it is hidden is a necessary part of its being hidden.[5]

Perhaps the meaning of the language of the material world is hidden, yet Beasley finds himself unable to cease exploring its possible meanings and analogues. This suggests that for Beasley there is not a *dearth* of meaning in the language of the material, but rather a superabundance, such that continued exploration will yield even more meaning, though always remaining incomplete and paradoxical. (In an epigraph to one of the poems, Beasley quotes the scientist Niels Bohr: "How wonderful that we have met with a paradox. Now we have some hope of making progress."[6]) Or perhaps, like our human languages, the natural world is not inherently meaningful, but can be made meaningful. Our world provides an unending host of objects and situations of which we might make meaning by analogy—by metaphor. Beasley's poems seem to acknowledge both of these possibilities, and much of their power derives from this tension.

The language of the material world for Beasley is simultaneously meaning-laden and unsoundable, and the same is true of human language and human spiritual speculation via the mechanism of language. Likewise, the material world provides analogues for the human spiritual or existential condition, as does our own language. These are the fundamental reasons that Beasley is so deeply engaged in wordplay—"play" that is for him a very serious matter indeed.

Beasley is clearly fascinated with the etymologies of words, and in his exploration of the revelatory possibilities of language he employs rarely used words, specialized vocabulary (primarily from science and religion), and neologisms. Consider the following words used in *Theophobia*: *paedomorphic, bibliolater, retrotransposon, obliquitous, unparousial, scatomancer, hematopoiesis, theomorphic, oneirotrope*. I have to keep a dictionary handy when reading Beasley's work, but for me there is pleasure and reward in examining etymologies along with the poet, as they serve to enhance the experience of the already engaging poems.

In the earlier excerpt from "Extremophilic Magnificat," for instance, we get a glimpse of some of Beasley's brilliant and deep linguistic wit. Chances are the reader will not recognize the word "eurytheotic." My interpretation is that it's a neologism that plays on the word "eurythermal," which means *able to tolerate a wide range of temperatures*—a characteristic of the Pompeii

5. Beasley, ix.
6. Ibid., 17.

worm described in this poem. So "eurytheotic" means something like *able to tolerate a wide range of divinity* or *able to tolerate a wide range of gods.* This word-play furthers the analogy between the physical attributes of the creatures in the poem and the speaker's spiritual state.

Here is another example of Beasley's wordplay, which is musical as well as significant:

> Glossolalic and disincarnate, interfere
> in me, interleave me
> and leave me through my breathing: like some third
>
> person conjugation I've rewhispered
> in a language I keep trying to learn, a tongue
> made only of verbs, and all its verbs irregular.[7]

We see here the recurring metaphor of God as language. Sound familiar? The material world as language; the self as language; God as language. For Beasley, in keeping with the Christian tradition which describes God as Word (see John 1), language is the central and all-encompassing metaphor.

> Me and You
> are like heterographs:
> the difference, say,
> between the sound of the g in God
> and the one in naught.[8]

However, all language available to us ultimately fails to articulate or enlighten our human dilemmas. We see this futility expressed when Beasley writes, "For the zeroth time I have told you what I mean,"[9] and in "Valedictions": "Are the utterative possibilities already exhausted / Do even questions leave // not anymore their mark."[10]

So why continue to use and explore the possibilities and limits of human language, and of the language of the material world? For Beasley, it is the imperfection of language, and our attempt at articulation in spite of that fact, that speaks most deeply and truly of who we are. Indeed, it is in the failures of our language—in our inarticulateness, in our confusion—that we come closest to what is holy:

---

7. Ibid., "Having Read the Holy Spirit's Wikipedia," 12.

8. Ibid., "Pilgrim's Deviations 2," 23.

9. Ibid., "Pilgrim's Deviations 6," 77.

10. Ibid., 39.

What is the Kingdom of God like? Like

(go in with your sickle)
a dim scriptorium

where many-written & half-hearted words
are mouthed beyond all attention,
swan quill stilled, dripping with gall & lampblack

ink. As if there were permissible
transcriptions of inattention,

missals riddled with elisions

to mark them aside (as if
in wax & urine & honey's

gold emblazing)

as unscriptable & dumbfounded: twice-blessed.[11]

In reading Bruce Beasley's work, I find myself in the presence of an intimidatingly broad intelligence—one that not only has a great store of knowledge but also makes associative leaps and linguistic ventures that probably would never have occurred to me. It is for that very reason that intimidation is replaced by curiosity, and curiosity accompanied by wonder. Here are poems that carry me along when I can't keep up, and which pull me close in moments of frightening intimacy. Here are uncomfortable poems that feel as familiar as my own doubting mind. Here is beauty marred with hectic pace that reminds me of the churnings of my own soul. Here is a poetry deeply rewarding to those of us who, like Beasley, wrestle with the metaphysical implications of our world and our lives in it.

11. Ibid., "As in a Dim Scriptorium," 71.

The Soul's Country

A review of Patrice de la Tour du Pin's
Psalms of All My Days, translated by Jennifer Grotz

Psalms of All My Days by Patrice de la Tour du Pin, translated by Jennifer Grotz (Carnegie Mellon University Press, 2013) (bilingual French/English)

The name Patrice de la Tour du Pin will be unfamiliar to a great number of English-language readers, and we are indebted to Jennifer Grotz for bringing his work into English for the first time. I first learned about De la Tour du Pin when I encountered some of Grotz's translations in a periodical. When I read the lines "If my dream is laughable, Lord, / extinguish it, for it consumes me!"[1] I was struck with the force of revelation—not of universal truth or of unknown information, but of access to another's experience of life, to its singular anguish and ecstasy. What T. S. Eliot said of George Herbert's work is relevant also to De la Tour du Pin's:

> When I claim a place for Herbert among those poets whose work every lover of English poetry should read and every student of English poetry should study, irrespective of religious belief or unbelief, I am not thinking primarily of the exquisite craftmanship, the extraordinary metrical virtuosity, or the verbal felicities, but of the *content* of the poems which make up *The Temple*. These poems form a record of spiritual struggle which should touch the feeling, and enlarge the understanding of those readers also who hold no religious belief and find themselves unmoved by religious emotion. (italics Eliot's)[2]

1. De la Tour du Pin, "Psalm 6," 43.
2. Eliot, 239.

It is not so much the stylistic or formal accomplishment of the work that makes it so enduring and vital, but rather the content itself—the experience communicated to the reader. Don't many of us believe, after all, that art in its highest function elicits empathy and incites the nobler instincts that lead us to value the other? De la Tour du Pin's work offers a fascinating and intense vicarious experience of the spiritual life of a poet who feels called to create a great lifework for his God, but who unrelentingly doubts that very endeavor.

De la Tour du Pin was born in 1911 and published his first poem in the prestigious *Nouvelle Revue Française* at the age of 20. He studied law at the École de Sciences Politiques in Paris, and served in the military during World War II. He was taken prisoner by the Germans and was released in 1942. The rest of his life was devoted to poetry, thanks to the auspices of his aristocratic family. Over a 30-year period, he worked on a 1,500-page multi-genre work entitled *Somme de Poésie*, in which his psalms were interspersed. In his late years, he was invited by the Catholic Church, after Vatican II, to assist in the composition of the French Catholic liturgy. In 1974, the year before his death, he published his psalms, revised and selected, in a separate volume, *Psaumes de tous mes jours*, with a foreword. The bilingual edition under review is a selection from that volume, with the addition of three early lyric poems.

De la Tour du Pin wrote his psalms out of an inner compulsion fierce enough to overcome the poet's own misgivings about the value and relevance of his work in an increasingly secular society. His mode and ideas were in direct opposition to the dominant Modernist literary culture of his time, and in fact the poems often explicitly address the dilemma of writing against the grain of cultural fashion and expectation. Consider his "Psalm 21":

> When they hear me sing my stubble fields, my little hills,
> they tell me: It's make-believe!
>
> Spending your life drawing your own soul's country,
> unconcerned with what's most serious.
>
> Your God is like your lapwings or elms:
> scanning the horizon, one finds nothing there.
>
> My God, don't leave me without a response:
> you whom I seek are not nothing.

I know all too well my footing's unstable,
but where is the man who doesn't straddle an abyss?

Those who hide this fact labor on artifice,
it's their network of ideas that is "make-believe."

I sing without even a thread to cushion my fall,
only the repetition of my breath supports me.

It pauses for a flight of lapwings above the bare fields
and my heart beats so hard it thinks it's flying.

At the pair of elm trees isolated upon the hill,
there he is, with me on my path.

My quest may be nothing to the experts,
but for me, it's to approach him by his own creation.

There are many layers in the depths of man,
and my God is the God who made them.

Through my spirit, he works the clay
and everything that rises from it speaks his Name.[3]

Knowing that he would seem foolish to others, De la Tour du Pin nevertheless persisted throughout his life in writing psalms of praise, lament, and
spiritual struggle, addressed at times to the reader, at times to a God in
whom he knew his audience likely did not believe. Unlike his poetic pre-
decessors, the Old Testament psalmists and the 17th-century Metaphysical poets, who also felt compelled to engage with their spiritual struggles
through their writing, De la Tour du Pin also had to come to terms with
the fact that he was writing amidst the rise of secularism, particularly in the
literary, artistic, and philosophical realms, in 20th-century Europe. What
makes these poems powerful even today is the persistence of the poet's devotion, his continual "quest" to present his "soul's country," so that even a
reader who does not share his belief might vicariously experience the poet's
religious passion and the vicissitudes of his spiritual experience.

As Grotz notes in her introduction, De la Tour du Pin wrote in his
foreword:

---

3. De la Tour du Pin, 77–79.

My first reaction at seeing [my psalms] reassembled here is a certain uneasiness. It is quite dangerous to speak so much about God, to repeat continually his Name! One exposes oneself so easily to the risk of irritating, annoying, or provoking reflections primarily in terms of psychology or literary history, whereas for the author these terms hardly count in and of themselves and what he wanted was precisely to absorb them into an even more complete synthesis![4]

These misgivings frequently appear in the poems themselves. Sometimes they take the form of self-scrutiny, an investigation of motives and character, concern about pride, as in "Psalm 1":

> yes, I loved greatness too much.
> I threw myself into the passion of writing;
> I savored the disgust of the vulgar.[5]

and "Psalm 2":

> Must we call it pride, this ambition to make a world,
> the spiritual delight in its shaping?
>
> [...]
> [Y]es, I admit it, I loved myself in poetry.
>
> Was it really just loving myself?
> nothing attracts me to myself when I undress.
>
> You alone understand this play that compels me
>   to its end,
> you alone can save me from it—or save it.[6]

and in "Psalm 6":

> Then I came to the dream of writing
> the great prayer of our time . . .
>
> This ambition plagues me constantly:
> I could never have the right to such a voice.
>
> [...]

4. Ibid., 13.

5. Ibid., 33.

6. Ibid., 35.

> If my dream is laughable, Lord,
> extinguish it, for it consumes me.
>
> It guides me in what I seek:
> could poetry be a kind of grace?
>
> I hold on to this lovely hope
> more tenacious at times than my demons.[7]

Other times, De la Tour du Pin doubts the ability of art to accomplish what he dreams, as well as his ability to adequately relate to the divine:

> If I exalt you, Lord, it's with words that perish,
> that fall back down on me like leaves in winter.[8]

And:

> I waste my efforts translating the ineffable:
> my rendering of life will never achieve clarity.
>
> Who would believe in my caverns, in my trees?
> Who will take my stones for real?[9]

In this last instance, we see the same trope as in "Psalm 21," the spiritual life of the poet as a landscape: lapwings, stubble-fields, caverns, trees. In this recurring figure, the poet is a painter attempting to depict something believable as "real," but which the viewer finds laughably fantastic and childish—"make-believe" ("Psalm 21"). But the spiritual existence De la Tour du Pin is attempting to portray is so natural, so organic for him that he has no way of keeping it out of his art:

> I am the only one who doesn't find
> my secret ambition ridiculous.
>
> I admit it out loud in order to cure myself
> but my God, it resurfaces each time I reject it.
>
> It says to the trees: you are not beyond my grasp,
> I hold vegetal mystery like you.
>
> To the animals deep in the forest or the sea:
> does not man contain all of you within himself?

7. Ibid., 43.
8. Ibid., "Psalm 7," 47.
9. Ibid., "Psalm 18," 71–73.

And to you whom I have never glimpsed above,
    you angels,
should I keep quiet about you as if you weren't there?

With my voice I raise up a body made of poetry,
I exhale in my breath everything that populates me.[10]

The poet does not so much inhabit a spiritual land as be inhabited by it. There is a touching sense of powerlessness here in the face of the divine, and one senses the poet's conflict about the fate chosen for him:

Why did you burden me with such a desire to praise
before you made me an angel,
why invest in someone who must be torn apart?[11]

Ultimately, De la Tour du Pin's poems are animated by a deep interior experience of connection with the divine. They bring the reader into the landscape where the poet walks, argues with, and finally embraces his God. And perhaps in that country of the soul, the reader—believer or not—will be moved with compassion, with empathy, and with—most significantly of all—recognition:

I will suspect myself, whatever I say;
and alone with you? I will only say *there you are*.

[. . .]

The two of us! most intimate, most free—
the call and response are the same.

Two of us! the heart and its secret.
Two of us: the throat and the voice to say so.[12]

These psalms of turmoil give the reader a way to feel something perhaps undreamed of, yet fully human for all its foreignness. There is wisdom in the saying that the particular is what makes art universal. And for any who may share the same kind of spiritual struggle as De la Tour du Pin, these psalms will offer assurance that they are not alone, that their experience is not alien to humanity. In either case, the ultimate function of these

10. Ibid., "Psalm 23," 85.
11. Ibid., "Psalm 33," 107.
12. Ibid., "Psalm 82," 139–141.

psalms is that which Joseph Conrad described when he wrote of the artist appealing to "the latent feeling of fellowship with all creation—and to the subtle but invincible conviction of solidarity that knits together the loneliness of innumerable hearts, to the solidarity in dreams, in joy, in sorrow, in aspirations, in illusions, in hope, in fear, which binds men [sic] to each other, which binds together all humanity—the dead to the living and the living to the unborn."[13]

13. Conrad, 120.

Paradise Re-Lost

A Review of Claudia Emerson's *Late Wife*

Late Wife by Claudia Emerson (Louisiana State University Press, 2005)

> It had to have come up from the cool underbelly
> of the first old house we rented, climbing
> pipes like branches to make a nest of the rusty
> sink-cabinet drawer where I kept the silverware.
> I opened it, and the snake lay coiled, brooding
> on its bed of edges—blades and tines....
> [...]
>   ...I let the snake
> escape, drain back into the house, and for years
> I told at that same table what I had to tell,
> how it disappeared the way it came.[14]

With these lines from the first poem in the collection, Claudia Emerson's *Late Wife* thrusts the reader immediately into a familiar but freshly-rendered postlapsarian world in which the natural world inevitably insinuates itself into the house, the human-made dwelling, and sometimes also finds a home there, though the human occupants remain ill-at-ease with its presence. There are spiders and termites, for instance, in "Rent" ("spiders—seasonless—survived the broom / to live in every corner," and a queen termite "pale and thick / as my thumb, invalid, being fed the house"[15]); in "Waxwing," a bird takes up temporary residence in the house, then is released after several weeks ("What had we saved // for a world so alien, the waxwing

---

14. Emerson, "Natural History Exhibits," 1–2.
15. Ibid., 7.

I must have believed it had died in those rooms...?"[16]); in "Metaphor," a bat enters the house, and the speaker's husband kills it ("I wanted // you to do it—until you did."[17]). Many of the poems in this book, primarily in the first of the three sections, but also throughout, are built on this primal dilemma of recognizing our connection to the natural world while defending ourselves against its encroachment into the house, the human-made space. For this reason, the speaker in the opening poem allows the snake to lie on the silverware, but vigorously washes all of it once the snake has moved—and the speaker later regrets not having killed it ("I know now I should have killed the snake"[18]). But she did not kill it, and it has sunk back into the house. And indeed, if Emerson had not allowed the snake, sinister and at home in the bowels of the house, to live in the poem, to dwell in the interstices of the house, there would be no book and we would be deprived of its sorrow and its moments of contentment, of its grotesque beauty and its harrowing truths.

To frame the book this way is to postpone discussing the book's more obvious subject and storyline. In the aftermath of Eden, it would seem, the speaker of these poems endures a divorce, then marries a man whose first wife has died. The second of the book's three sections combines explorations of the psychological upheaval caused by the speaker's divorce with evocative reminiscences from her childhood. The third section, however, is the most subtle and formally deft of the three. It opens with a sonnet that explores the primary motif of the book: the house and the objects that make up the household. Many of the poems thus far have dealt with the speaker's houses, but now "Artifact" deals with her new husband's house, along with the objects he has kept from the house he once shared with his late wife:

> . . . and the quilt you spread on your borrowed bed—
> small things. Months after we met, you told me she had
> made it, after we had slept already beneath its loft
> and thinning, raveled pattern, as though beneath
> her shadow, moving with us, that dark, that soft.[19]

16. Ibid., 10.
17. Ibid., 17.
18. Ibid., "Natural History Exhibits," 2.
19. Ibid., 41.

And the rest of the book does indeed move beneath the shadow of her death, along with the shadow of the speaker's divorce—two smaller shadows within the great shadow of The Fall itself. Whereas the speaker's marriage seems to have ended because of frustration in the relationship, her new husband remained devoted to his first wife to the end. This lends great psychological complexity to this section, so that when the speaker's husband tells her about his first wife's illness or when her possessions show up—a daybook, a photograph, a glove—the reader feels the speaker's conflicting emotions. The speaker desires to know who this woman was, and perhaps even to love her somehow as well, since she was beloved, but this task is ultimately impossible, so there is a gulf that remains between her and her husband. The speaker must also feel confusion as she lives with someone who loves her, but will never stop loving a former wife as well. In "Old English," one of the finest poems in the collection, the book's many strands coalesce in the space of seven lines:

> I buried the sheepdog for you, trying
> to save you from that grief, dug through muscled
> roots, past rain-wet earth to harder, drier
> soil that did not cling, but scoured the shovel.
>
> Even the expected, smaller death recalled
> the other. I transplanted sedum from the garden
> to mark the place and obscure it.[20]

In context of this third section, the reader will emphasize the word "that" in the second line far more than one normally might, which lends emotional potency to the line. Again, in context of the section and of the book, "the other" death referred to in the second stanza must refer not only to the husband's first wife's death, but also to the entrance of death itself into the world in Genesis. And finally, a plant is brought out of the garden to paradoxically "mark" the place and to "obscure" (both darken and hide) it. This is a post-Edenic setting in which the natural world is both kept at bay and tended, a world in which beautiful plants feed on the rotting flesh of beloved animals and in which relationships are predicated on loss.

Before judging this collection to work within too familiar territory, one would do well to read it through. Emerson casts her narrative within the ancient allegory of The Fall with formal deftness, tonal subtlety, and psychological acuity, such that the reader can almost hear the flaming

20. Ibid., 52.

sword guarding the entrance to Eden flicking back and forth in the distance, as if that blade were the source of the light in which these poems cast their shadows.

Masterful Variations

A Review of Ashley Anna McHugh's
Into These Knots

Into These Knots by Ashley Anna McHugh (Ivan R. Dee, 2010)

In Ashley Anna McHugh's "All Other Ground Is Sinking Sand" ("On Christ the solid rock I stand" goes the previous line of the hymn this title is taken from), a villanelle addressed to the speaker's father, we find ourselves at the ailing father's bedside and learn that he has a bedsore that has turned gangrenous:

> Doctors say that he could die: They have to hurry,
> might amputate. He nods, then the click of the door,
> and my father cries, he prays—but this is a hard story:
>
> Staph spreads, and surgeons treat his body like a quarry.
> Close to his spine, they mine the green-black ore—
> and still, he prays. I can't—but this is my father's story.
> So, Thine be the kingdom. Thine, the power. Thine, the glory.[21]

Here, at the end of the poem, we see McHugh's command of form in full force. When I say *form*, I don't only mean the metrical framework (in this case, predominantly hexameter, uncommon in English-language villanelles) or the repeating pattern of the villanelle; I also mean McHugh's masterful variations of syntax, punctuation, even typography, all of which enable this poem, whose dramatic situation is already emotionally fraught, to achieve a level of emotional impact that would be impossible in the hands of a poet of lesser ability. In this short poem (five tercets and a quatrain), there are six colons, one semicolon, and three em dashes. As is evident in the above excerpt, the use of these "hard" punctuation marks, in addition to

21. McHugh, 14.

all the periods, allows the poem to progress in uncertain fits and starts, in staccato time. This effect increases at the close of the poem so that in the last line alone we encounter three periods and three commas. What's more, the initial repeating line of the poem—which, in McHugh's oh-so-slight variation on the dictates of the villanelle form, serves as the closing line of the poem rather than the penultimate—began as a complete phrase from the King James version of what is commonly called "The Lord's Prayer," unimpeded by punctuation: "*Thine be the kingdom and the power and the glory.*" As the poem progresses, it gets shortened first to "*Thine the power, and the glory,*" and then finally it is expanded again, but rhythmically chopped even further into fragments: "So, Thine be the kingdom. Thine, the power. Thine, the glory." Here, where the speaker has adopted the father's prayer as her own despite her lack of faith, the italics have disappeared. This is no longer merely a quotation—from the Bible, from the speaker's father—but the prayer has become, somehow, paradoxically, her own. McHugh has given us a powerful, compact exploration of faith's link to love, of the way devotion leads to devotion—devotion to her father moving the speaker toward the divine.

I should also note McHugh's remarkable ability to make metaphor, as when "the surgeons treat his body like a quarry." Too many poets would be content with having found an interesting rhyme (*phew*!) that also provided an interesting metaphor and would have moved on. But McHugh senses how artificial that would feel in the context of this story, and so the metaphor is extended and explored through the next line, so that the aptness of the comparison becomes more clear: "Close to his spine, they mine the green-black ore." This metaphor not only conveys a sense of the father becoming an inanimate object upon which the doctors act (one effect of medical terminology, perhaps, and more literally embodied in surgery under anesthesia), but the metaphor also conveys the idea of value—a mine for precious ore.

In this poem we see the technical strengths that are everywhere evident in McHugh's first book as well as her primary thematic concerns: a conflicted exploration of her religious upbringing and meditations on intimate relationships, both familial and romantic. McHugh achieves admirable tonal variety in these poems, though one difficulty that results from this variety is that in the first section humorous, relatively frivolous lyrics sit uneasily beside poems about dying loved ones and the suicidal. Between "Ashes on Assateague Island," with such lines as

> And now the nurses ease
> the tubes from your wrists, the wires from your chest.
> I send you through the fire.[22]

and "Song for the Suicidal," where we read

> Where the hooded man crouched, rocking.
> Nurses snatched her hand.
> Where the pale boys shuffled cards.
> She wore a numbered band.[23]

come several poems, including "From His Coy Mistress," a response to Marvell's famous poem, ending with these lines:

> Rolling our strength and sweetness to a ball
> took fifteen minutes, maybe, at the best.
>
> So gentlemen, fill me in: If there's not time
> for decent sex, how's coyness such a crime?[24]

This is a wonderful bit of tongue-in-cheek, but the placement in the collection makes the wit at work seem mere comic relief and diminishes the effect of both the humorous and the grave poems in the section.

The central sequence of the collection, "Cairns," a 17-part poem in rhyming pentameter, tells the story of a man, Jake, remembering a hiking trip with his now-dead father through West Virginia land where old explosives left by the military have been marked with cairns (heaps of rocks). The catalyst of Jake's memory is lilac petals swarming in a pre-storm wind:

> Maybe he can let the past be past
>
> if the lilacs settle, still their frantic stir?
> Become what they are instead of what they were?[25]

These petals frame the sequence. By the time they reappear in the last section of the poem, we have learned much about Jake's relationship with his father and the way the volatility of the explosives encountered on their hike has come to symbolize that relationship for Jake. Here is section XIII:

> He'd tripped, and then he felt the cairn divide.

22. Ibid., 15.
23. Ibid., 19.
24. Ibid., 17.
25. Ibid., 26.

Three rocks. Cairn as warning, not a guide.
Bright shell. Nothing was hurt, and nothing died.
He knew this should have been enough of luck.

It wasn't. His father unfolded maps, and wrote
the landmarks, guessed the distance to the road.
Rebuilt the cairn. They hiked on east, their route
unchanged. They followed blazes: Cairn to cairn.

Cairns as warnings, as guides: across the river,
when hard-packed trail gave way to brush, or over
rock fields—. At every cairn, his heart would shiver.
Then: Tree-line. Fist of wind. Air thin. Then: Dark.

He closed his eyes. Shell after shell. He thought
his father gasped back there, but maybe not.[26]

The sequence moves back and forth in time, painting scenes at home, on the trail, at the hospital, and finally one in which Jake is building a cairn as a memorial to his father, the wind blowing through it:

No cairn will answer it: No trail. No shell.
Nothing to follow,
                            nothing to fear—but wind
whinnies its cracks, and so it howls, sings sharp:
it names itself with the song of an empty sign . . . .[27]

The sections of "Cairns" are placed solidly at the center of this book, form-ing, if you will, a cairn of words that does justice to the character's own attempt to understand and memorialize his father.

The final section of the collection, like the first, assembles poems on the themes of love, death, and religion. One of the most effective poems of this section, "Hunting Accident," recalls the first poem of the book, which warns, "Beware the favor of God," and tells the story of the speaker's father dying in a fall from a tree-stand, praying for mercy before he died, receiving Job's response from God:

[M]y father fell, and splintered his spine.
Half-buried by leaves, he prayed
for mercy—for an answer, a sign.

26. Ibid., 33.
27. Ibid., 42.

From deep in that whirlwind,
God gave His reason: *Who gave birth*
to the hoarfrost of heaven?
And from whose womb did the ice come forth?[28]

"Hunting Accident" seems to be about the same incident, but interestingly it shifts halfway through to focus on a shot deer from the past:

. . . its unfocused

eyes diluted   and uncertain, almost
alive—a second   shot, then the lull,
like a cradle. Becoming   meat is so simple.[29]

Again, we see McHugh's formal acuity at work. The caesuras imposed by whitespace work marvelously well here, lending the force of breath stopped then released to the word "shot" and providing suggestions of multiple connotations for the phrases "like a cradle. Becoming" and "meat is so simple."

The complexities of the relationships and ideas in *Into These Knots* are served well by the precision and ingenuity of McHugh's formal techniques. This is an extraordinary debut marked by aesthetic and emotional effects achieved through formal mastery, and we can look forward eagerly to McHugh's future books.

28. Ibid., "Deer Hunting," 3–4.
29. Ibid., 54.

Writing From a Life

A Review of Carl Phillips' *Riding Westward*

Riding Westward by Carl Phillips (Farrar, Straus and Giroux, 2007)

Carl Phillips has long written poems that ignore contemporary American aesthetic doctrines, and that fact in itself is heartening. He is entirely comfortable with abstraction, often building his poems on lofty language, and he is unafraid to "tell" as much as he "shows." His tone is that of one speaking to an intimate about shared experience, without the kind of sarcasm we often call irony. Consequently, the poems tend to allude to experiences in a fragmentary way, as if the reader has prior knowledge of them and needs only small reminders. What is more, the reader is seldom sure where or when the situation described by one of Phillips' poems is occurring. Because of these qualities, the poems in Phillips' collection *Riding Westward* may at first confound readers who are used to so-called accessible poetry. In fact, "accessibility" is one of those contemporary doctrines I mentioned above—one which Phillips thankfully ignores. The following lines from "Erasure," the first poem in the collection, are a good example of these qualities:

> Above us, the usual branches lift unprophetically or not, depending:
> now spears; now arrows. There's a kind of tenderness that makes
> more tender
>
>   all it touches. There's a need that ruins. Dark. The horse
> comes closer. [...][1]

Here, we have "the usual branches," as if they are usual not only to the speaker of the poem (and to the "him" mentioned earlier in it), but to the

---

1. Phillips, 3.

reader as well. We have fragments of a scene: branches lifting, darkness, a horse referred to with a definite article as if we already knew it was there—but the scene remains fragmentary throughout the poem, and we never quite know where or when we are situated. The above lines also illustrate Phillips' propensity to "tell" as well as "show," his refusal to shirk from making authoritative pronouncements: "There's a need that ruins," and "There's a kind of tenderness that makes more tender // all it touches." However, the tone of this poem is quite complicated, because not only are we assumed to understand this fragmentary scene, but we are presented with a speaker who makes both authoritative statements and equivocations: "the usual branches lift unprophetically or not"—an equivocation intensified by the double-negative construction. Double negatives recur throughout the collection, working as semantic counterbalances to the authoritative tone of the speakers of the poems, as their logical clumsiness has the effect of undermining what might otherwise seem effortless pronouncements.

Another potentially disorienting aspect of these poems is the fact that the titles often have nothing overtly to do with the poems or their dramatic situations. There is "Bright World," which does not describe brightness at all, or even the world very much; there is "The Way Back," which is about "the urge to make meaning"[2]; there is "The Smell of Hay," which is about memory, but mentions no situation involving either hay or the sense of smell; there is "The Cure," which describes a dying tree, which ends up as a metaphor for history, and light falling through it, a metaphor for human lives—but no sign of a cure anywhere for the dying tree or the human lives tumbling through its branches. These are only a few examples of titles that are not linked to their poems the way we typically expect them to be, since they are not descriptive of the poems' content. Instead, the titles function evocatively: their effect is to create mood by association. In the same way, these poems are anything but descriptive of the world or of life—they do not set out to paint a clear picture of the world or of experiences, as we have largely come to expect poems to do. Phillips' poems are far too abstract and fragmentary to do that. But they do something equally important by letting the reader's imagination participate more fully with the speakers of the poems. While reading this collection, one often repositions oneself imaginatively in order to create, along with the poem, the story to which the poem alludes. The fact that this is effective is a testimony to the power of this collection—it is not something a lesser poet could achieve.

2. Ibid., 8.

One way to describe Phillips' poems is to acknowledge that they function more evocatively than descriptively. What I mean is that they are not by any means *about* life, which would be no accomplishment at all; rather, they are *of* life, out of it, and convincingly so, which is a great accomplishment indeed. His poems are informed by and allude to experience without having to entirely create or recreate it, and this is the source of their authority. In "Turning West," Phillips himself makes a similar distinction when he mentions "a distance like that between writing *from* a life / and writing *for* one . . . " (Phillips' italics).[3] Writing for a life might mean writing in order to have a life, to create one out of a paucity of living or being present in the world. This is decidedly not the kind of writing Phillips does. It is clear that his poems are *from* life. The evidence of this is the powerful effect they have on the reader who is willing to lay aside expectations for simply "accessible" poetry and who is willing to imaginatively engage, as with an intimate, in these evocative, allusive conversations.

3. Ibid., 36.

A Second Experience

A Review of Two Books by
Stella Vinitchi Radulescu

Stella Vinitchi Radulescu:

Insomnia in Flowers (Plain View Press, 2008)

Diving with the Whales (March Street Press, 2008)

Novice poets often make the mistake of putting most of their effort into evoking the *feeling* of experience rather than first practicing a more objective, concrete description of experience. If something is highly emotional, highly subjective, then to them it automatically qualifies as good poetry. They don't realize it yet, but they are trying to take a shortcut to eliciting emotion in the reader. If the poem contains an overabundance of emotion, then how can the reader not have an emotional experience? The problem is that witnessing emotion or being told about emotion is not at all the same as having an emotional response to a firsthand experience. And I don't think, when it comes to poetry, that this is a failure of sympathy. What happens is that, without a participatory experience on the reader's part, any emotion in the poem is likely to remain unconvincing at best, or to seem like a gimmick at worst. The inexperienced poet does not yet understand that it is impossible to create emotion without creating experience for the reader—and that is precisely what all good poetry must do, rather than simply chronicling an emotional response to some other experience. The experience that a poem creates may be of any kind: realistic, fantastic, linguistic, rhetorical, philosophical, propositional, etc., etc. But if the poet is unaware of the need to create an experience of one kind or another for the reader, he or she is not likely to succeed very often at doing so, merely by chance.

What Stella Vinitchi Radulescu does most expertly is to create an experience for the reader of her poems. The nature of the experience of reading her poems is most often surrealistic, achieved in a sparse, fragmentary style. In many of Radulescu's poems, she is also concerned with creating a meta-level linguistic experience. Many of her poems do chronicle emotional responses to various life experiences, but she writes her poems with the inherent understanding that they must create a second experience that is not merely a retelling of the original. The opening poem of Radulescu's collection, *Insomnia in Flowers*, is a fine example of this:

> a room
> in the room
> my flesh in yours   thank you mother
>
> thanks for taking me back   for the fresh leaves
> the language I speak once a year when the sun
>
> digs you out   cherry trees in blossom again
> rehearsing a new death
> spelling loud your silence
> a short yes
> flowers for teeth
>
> teeth for flowers[1]

What we can notice about Radulescu's poem is that it is not a retelling of experience, but a distillation of experience. Thus the fragmentary images and thoughts—only those things that will be most vital for the reader's second experience. She is also unafraid of defying the original experience for the sake of the second; in other words, she makes something new out of the material of the original experience, and is willing, even eager, to shape and distort the raw material. This way, she achieves a surrealistic effect, conflating the cherry trees with the mother, such that the blossoms begin by "spelling loud" the silence of the dead mother—simply reminding the speaker of her mother and of her death—and then morph to actually take on her physical characteristics, to *become* her: "flowers for teeth / / teeth for flowers." I would contend that this second experience the reader has is not the same experience the poet (or the speaker of the poem) had, and yet, perhaps *because* the poem is not an attempt to simply recreate the same

---

1. Radulescu, *Insomnia . . .* , "Spelling Loud," 7.

experience, and it is also not an attempt to convey emotion divorced from an experience of the reader's own, it succeeds in conveying the emotional quality of the original.

Other poems of Radulescu's seem less likely to have arisen from a single identifiable original experience, and yet are no less adept in creating an experience for the reader. We can see this in "Scream," which I reproduce here in its entirety:

> I went too far, too far in the woods. The tree
> was there, the body hanging
> from a branch.
>
> It was yesterday, I was looking for God.
>
> Free from gravity, his legs in the wind
> right, left . . .
> a creepy balance between shadows and light.
>
> Too far on Earth, too far into night . . . I touched
> the corpse, it went away in flames
> and dust.
>
> He is still here in the declining moon some words would fit
> his skull
>
> And I was scared, the scream
> took my whole body with it, I thought I was flying . . .
>
> But no, there I found myself stuck on the ground
> from scream to scream building
> an altar of silence.[2]

This poem is more propositional than "Spelling Loud." Even the fact that there are capital letters, as there rarely are in Radulescu's poems, indicates that this is a narrative, discursive mode, rather than primarily an imagistic mode. Here, we have the idea of mystical pursuit taken too far. The poem seems to indicate that seeking God can be dangerous, when one is attempting to exceed the bounds of human knowledge and experience. And yet, the traumatic experience ultimately results in worship: "from scream to scream building / an altar of silence." In this poem, Radulescu is proposing

2. Ibid., 11.

an idea rather than simply recounting an experience, and yet it is through the reader's imaginative experience of the dreamlike scene described that the idea arrives so forcefully and so convincingly.

Oftentimes, in true Surrealist form, Radulescu's poems ask the reader to see combinations and juxtapositions of things that would not be possible in "the real world." These surrealistic images and scenes create yet another kind of experience, akin to that in "Spelling Loud," and yet distinct, because the surrealism in that poem can be read as psychological metaphor. It is not so easy to categorize other poems of hers this way. The final stanza of the poem "If I Remember," from *Diving with the Whales*, is a fine example:

> lavender evening
> ghosts approaching the shore
> I follow their footpath   I almost
> hit a star[3]

In "On Turtles and Death," from *Insomnia in Flowers*, Radulescu combines her fascination with language itself with her surrealistic style:

> the high tide leaves more verbs on the beach
> I draw them all over my feet   *they whisper*[4]

The title poem of *Insomnia in Flowers* contains these wonderful lines:

> my house floats backwards on the river
>
> a child in the garden opens
> black wings[5]

And Radulescu can be more playful as well, combining artistic or literary allusions to create unforgettable images:

> sky was a joke in our late conversation
> a man lighting his blue cigars
> with Stevens' tie[6]

It seems to me that Radulescu's basic concern is spiritual investigation, and carrying the reader along, to the extent possible, in her mystical pursuit. In "Starting Point," from *Diving with the Whales*, she writes about seeking

3. Radulescu, *Diving* . . . , 30.
4. *Insomnia* . . . , 70.
5. Ibid., 54.
6. Ibid., "Stars Are Like Children," 17.

understanding, and says, "and what if I fail and what if I don't,"[7] acknowledging the fearfulness of each possibility—either perpetual uncertainty, or revelation that is too much to bear (as in "Spelling Loud," quoted above). She goes on to say, in the third section of the poem:

> the answer is in our hands
> but we don't understand a long time ago
>
> we named things at random
> now we are paying for it
>
> we don't see a soul like we see the moon rising
> we don't understand simple facts
>
> where are we going
> why do the seagulls cry   I have these words
>
> sometimes I feel like touching their flesh
> the roundness
> and then I let them fall
> one by one into your mouth, Mr. Nothing
>
> make me an offer
> I will buy your big and burning eyes[8]

Those burning eyes of Mr. Nothing tell it all—Radulescu suspects that there really is no answer to the mystery of existence, no ultimate meaning. And yet, in personifying and speaking to that nothingness, the poem gives nothingness form and refuses to accept nihilism. The only way, for Radulescu, of approaching the mystery of existence is words themselves. Notice how she makes them tangible: "I have these words / sometimes I feel like touching their flesh . . . ." And then they become the bargaining chips with which she will "buy [the] big and burning eyes" of Mr. Nothing by dropping them into his mouth. Radulescu is skeptical, but unrelenting, in her pursuit of mystery through words. In her unrelentingness, she reminds me of the 17th-century Metaphysical poets and the mystics, while stylistically she is clearly a descendent of the Surrealists and Modernists. She has melded disparate traditions seamlessly in her poetry, and the precise mixture of elements in her work is perhaps unique in American poetry, and our poetry is

---

7. *Diving . . .* , 8.
8. Ibid., 8–9.

richer for it. Radulescu's poetry offers the reader powerful experiences by which one can participate in the mystical pursuit that is the fundamental characteristic of her work.

Ignorance and Awe

A Review of Stephen Haven's *Dust and Bread*

Dust and Bread by Stephen Haven (Turning Point, 2008)

Stephen Haven's *Dust and Bread* opens with an epigraph from Emily Dickinson's poem #575: "An Awe if it should be like that / Upon the Ignorance steals—."[1] In this collection, Haven's poems present ignorance as a pathway to awe. The tourist or visitor is the primary metaphor in the first section of the book, a metaphor which resonates throughout the collection as a way of thinking about all situations in which one feels dislocated, unknowledgeable, or inexperienced. And in a larger sense, the metaphor comes to address the fundamental human condition.

In "Blossom," the speaker, an American visiting the Summer Palace in Beijing, wonders, "What can a tourist know? The past / is made of stone."[2] We are presented the humble tourist, one who acknowledges his limitations regarding a history and a culture other than his own. This is the model Haven would hold up for the reader as a paradigm for life in the broadest sense. Humility of this kind—a willingness to admit and accept ignorance—bears much resemblance to Keats' idea of negative capability. This collection can be seen as an explicit exploration of what Keats described as a capacity for "being in uncertainties, mysteries, doubts, without any irritable reaching after fact and reason."[3]

The first section of the book explores (presumably) Haven's own experience as an American visiting Beijing, which is the setting for deep complexities and conflicts in his experience of the world. In Beijing, he both witnesses the birth of his child and meditates on the Tiananmen Square

1. Haven, 7.
2. Ibid., 30.
3. Keats, *The Letters* . . . , 193–194.

massacre, which some members of his wife's family experienced firsthand. In "Ultrasound," Haven addresses his daughter while she is still in the womb, as her mother sings at her family's home:

> Only one young uncle falls asleep,
> his face gone purple with grief and baijiu,
>
> his one son lost shoveling coal
> at the Beijing Duck Hotel,
> then biking home, after dark, past
>
> Tiananmen, June 4th.
> Anniversary of absences,
> song of a night to be sad.
>
> Someone recalls, now, on his birthday,
> in prison, your mother's father was given
> one boiled goose egg.
>
> [. . .]
>
> [T]he moon refuses to show,
> masked in clouds and the earth's shadow,
> its power magnified behind a shroud.
>
> Begonias of violence, man-powered stars
> burst their last cartwheels
> in a long rumor of dawn.[4]

This is not a situation that begets certainty, and it is only within his experience of a conflicted world, in which he must ultimately admit ignorance, that any certainty arises. Here is the birth of his son (Haven's biographical statement says that he lives with his wife "and their many children"), a moment of revelation—but one which depends on accepting ignorance:

> we knew right then just what we were,
> knew it was religion,
> its work, its aspiration,
> the body broken, breaking,
> the blood poured out
> eternity itself—
> or something like it—

4. Haven, 18–19.

glinting in and out of view
in the double black-brown crystal,
the deep translucence
of a one-day old.[5]

This is one of the purest moments of awe in the collection, and awe is only possible when revelation is offered to one who waits in an attitude of humility and ignorance.

The collection moves through three additional sections, each, like the first, containing nine poems—a formal parallel to Beijing's Temple of Heaven, described in the first section as "a times table,"[6] the floor of each level made up of slabs in multiples of nine. Haven also flexes his formal muscle with a few poems in received form: a sestina, a couple poems in blank verse, and a villanelle. He moves seamlessly into and out of traditional form, and indeed, the sestina is one of the finest poems in the collection—a young boy's account of a Catholic bishop's three-day stay at his house during a snowstorm. The poem starts with a somewhat trepidatious tone, but then the bishop begins to seem like part of the household:

[S]omething uncommon was in our home,
where we dealt the Queen of Spades, dark cousin of
  the snow,
the Bishop in my father's robe, his new maroon pontificals.
We hoped it would snow and snow, that he wouldn't
  go away.[7]

A sestina requires the repetition of the end-words of each line in each stanza, but in a masterstroke of craftsmanship, Haven drops the word "pontificals" from the next, penultimate stanza (substituting "ponderous, fickle," no less!), because for the boy, the bishop is no longer a symbol of the church, but an actual person. The word "pontificals" returns in the final stanza, but only as "the shock of his pontificals" in the snow as he leaves the house—a shock not only because of color, but because the man has been dissociated from his church office in the boy's mind. This poem wonderfully describes a child's process of unlearning, of entering a state of blessed ignorance that allows him to see the Bishop as a *person* for the first time.

5. Ibid., "Another Genesis," 24.

6. Ibid., "Temple of Heaven," 25.

7. Ibid., "Snowed-in with the Bishop, Confirmation Day," 40.

Here, as throughout Haven's collection, we see the paradox of ignorance serving as a vital kind of knowledge.

The book's title comes from a wonderful poem, "Summer in a Large House," from the last section. Here, a woman who thinks she hears ghosts at night is comforted by her husband:

> [H]e held her when she asked, pressed into her
> the rote illusion of some distant mass,
> the only prayer he knew, of love and dust
> and bread, and she recited it after him
> though neither one could say to what or whom.
> And still it pulled, born of one breath
> that bent above them the cypress's silhouette
> and drifting, drifting, unseen everywhere,
> pitched forever, it seemed to them forever,
> dark and near in the warped old eaves of the ear.[8]

It is in the state of uncertainty, both acknowledged and confessed ("he held her when she asked"), that what might be called awe is possible—awe at finding oneself a part of something incomprehensible, unfathomable, about which one must admit ignorance; and awe at finding oneself with one—ultimately, with many—who are capable of sharing both the ignorance and the awe. *Dust and Bread* is clear evidence that Haven is learned in the ways of ignorance, and that ignorance itself has taught him an abundance of beautiful things, not the least of which being a receptivity to revelation and the awe that can attend it.

8. Ibid., 76.

A Kind of Grace

A Review of Morri Creech's *Field Knowledge*

Field Knowledge by Morri Creech (Waywiser Press, 2006)

Morri Creech's poetry is unabashedly a poetry for those who read. When he's not speaking of what seems to be his own life, he invades the consciousnesses of the dead or mythic. In various ways, he conjures Orpheus, Job and his wife, Primo Levi, Giotto, Leonardo DaVinci, Isaac Newton, Blake, Rousseau, Wordsworth, Keats, Marx, Matthew Arnold, and Simone Weil, among others. *Field Knowledge*, chosen by J. D. McClatchy for the 2005 Anthony Hecht Prize and nominated for the *Los Angeles Times* Book Award, certainly evinces knowledge of historical and literary fields, and assumes the same knowledge-base for its readers. Don't get me wrong—I find this refreshing. It seems in no way presumptuous to suppose that those who love poetry love to read. This assumption has only recently fallen away from poetry in a large-scale way. As J. D. McClatchy notes in the foreword, instead of reverting merely to "private memory," Creech "prefers more amplitude, and draws on a range of classical and biblical allusions, on the choreography of rhetoric, on the complexities of science and nature."[1] Creech's poetry, then, is distinct from much of what is written in America today. Yet, for all its learnedness, his poetry is not obscure or "difficult" in the pejorative sense.

Creech's primary field is not myth, or history, or literature—it is the human experience and the human condition. The "field," in fact, is a recurring image in this collection, symbolic of the world in which we all participate, at once physical and symbolic, difficult and beautiful, mundane and mythic. The field is the physical world acted upon, emblematic of the human drive to discover and to create significance. "Listening to the Earth,"

1. McClatchy, "Foreword," *Field Knowledge*, 12.

a poem reminiscent of Richard Wilbur's "Advice to a Prophet," imagines a people who are used to hearing the cries of a biblical prophet, and are, frankly, sick of it. But soon they begin to sense a loss, an emptiness. Here is the final stanza:

> And in the plain streets we listened
> for those syllables that once conjured the cold,
> fathomless swells of Leviathan-haunted seas,
> the fabled bush ablaze on hallowed ground,
> and snowflakes' mythic treasuries,
> transfiguring our ordinary fields.[2]

The task of the prophet is the task of the poet, the task that Creech takes up in his masterful second collection. Creech transfigures ordinary human fields—physical fields, as in the title poem, and figurative fields, as in "Some Notes on Grace and Gravity"—into messengers speaking specially for us. We would do well to listen, lest we forget the "things in which we have seen ourselves and spoken,"[3] as Richard Wilbur put it. If we attend closely, we may find, as Newton finds in Creech's book, that even "gravity [. . .] becomes a kind of grace."[4]

---

2. Creech, 38.

3. Wilbur, "Advice to a Prophet," 258.

4. Creech, "Some Notes on Grace and Gravity," 27.

The Poet and the Priest

A Review of Spencer Reece's
The Road to Emmaus

The Road to Emmaus by Spencer Reece (Farrar, Straus and Giroux, 2014)

Spencer Reece's second collection of poems, *The Road to Emmaus*, opens with a stunning poem describing his experience as a priest in a neonatal ICU, which ends:

> It is correct to love even at the wrong time.
> On rounds, the newborns eyed me, each one
> like Orpheus in his dark hallway, saying:
> *I knew I would find you, I knew I would lose you.*[1]

Here, Reece articulates a transcendent and devastating encounter with mortality that strikes the reader with both the perennial familiarity of myth and an arresting contemporary specificity. In the first line quoted above, Reece makes a rather grand philosophical statement, reminiscent of those found in the work of the late Jack Gilbert. Reece wisely uses this type of statement sparingly, as philosophical generalizations are so often problematic. (E.g., What does "correct" mean? What would it mean for a time to be "wrong" for love?) But by moving swiftly past this grandiloquent utterance into his visceral experience in the neonatal ICU, Reece implicitly asks the reader not to dwell on the semantics and technicalities of the statement, but to simply feel its resonance with the experience being described. And, as in the best of Jack Gilbert's work, that resonance is profound. The reader feels the *wrongness* in the fragility of life and unearned suffering of

---

1. Reece, "ICU," 3.

the newborns, and the *correctness* in the human attachment between the newborns and Reece.

Unfortunately, this poem remains unequalled until late in the collection (with the prose poem "Hartford: Visions"). That's not to say there isn't much to admire in the intervening poems, but the lyric intensity of the opening poem falls away for a meandering voice that sifts through the details of life, looking for those that are most significant. But the speaker can't seem to decide which are significant—or, when he does decide, why those should be the significant ones.

Reece is a gay Episcopalian priest, and in *The Road to Emmaus* he primarily explores what at least appears to be the poet's own past, including family history, friendships, romantic relationships, seminary, and priestly duties in such places as prisons and hospitals. The poems vary greatly in length and form: Shorter poems are interspersed with long poems—some well over 20 pages—and the forms he employs include free verse, rhymed couplets (in one poem), prose poems, and a sonnet. The strangest formal element in this collection is unpredictable, sporadic rhyme in some of the long free-verse poems. At times, these random rhymes make it seem as if Reece were poking fun at himself for writing poetry. Most of these rhymes feel overly obvious (*beach/each*, *right/light*, *phone/alone*), calling attention to the artifice of telling a story in poetry. These rhymes, when they appear, often ring with a faux childish note, like T. S. Eliot's in "The Love Song of J. Alfred Prufrock," and indeed, Reece's voice is often full of uncertainty and dismayed confusion, like Prufrock's.

In the title poem, one of the long free-verse poems, the speaker recounts what seems a quasi-romantic, though non-physical, relationship with a man he calls Durrell, whom he met at an AA group and who has died. "[W]herever I moved," the speaker says,

> we spoke,
> daily, over the phone, on landlines—
> talking and listening, listening and talking, for *fifteen* years:
> [. . .]
> In all that time, I only saw him once more,
> and by then he was nearly blind.
> In all that time, we barely touched one another.[2]

The setting for the retelling of this relationship is a series of counseling sessions with a nun, who has a postcard on her wall depicting Christ's

2. Ibid., "The Road to Emmaus," 65.

post-resurrection appearance to two disciples on the road to Emmaus, who fail to recognize him as the Christ until that evening as they eat together. In Reece's title poem, as throughout the collection, the speaker searches for God's presence in the daily, concrete reality of his life and relationships. The title of the book and the biblical story it references imply that the sacred is here with us, now, in each particular of our lives—and for the most part we fail to recognize that fact. Reece seems convinced that he has failed to comprehend the sacred significance of his life, like the disciples on the road to Emmaus, and so pores over the details of his past.

At times he seeks God outside everyday life, as in his two periods of seminary study:

> But I went in search of the transcendent in those days,
> which required leaving a particular world for another.
> It is never easy to abandon a world.
> It was my second attempt.[3]

Although he is never harshly critical of seminary or the cloistered religious life, Reece does depict such a life as overly removed from the world and as artificial: "Inside everyone sat, knelt, stood, and genuflected / with the informed hush of a troupe of mime artists."[4] And so it is ultimately in his priestly engagements with the outside world (in orphanages, hospitals, and prisons, for instance) and in his "secular" life that he finds transcendence. As he says about Durrell in "The Road to Emmaus," "All I know now / is the more he loved me, the more I loved the world."[5] It seems that the structure of the secular world, more than that of the church, is most spiritually meaningful to him. He writes about Miami, for instance: "How I love your decks, bridges, promenades, and balconies— / the paraphernalia of connection."[6] It is human connection that remains of utmost importance for Reece, and oftentimes his religious training seems useless to him in his engagements with others, as in "A Few Tender Minutes":

> Before me is a man who does not disclose his crime, a Native American who will be released tomorrow [. . .]. For forty years, he tells me, his job has been to greet new inmates, which gave him money for toothpaste and pencils. Behind him, a mural of

3. Ibid., "The Upper Room," 109.
4. Ibid., 114.
5. Ibid., "The Road to Emmaus," 69.
6. Ibid., "The Prodigal Son," 78.

crude voluptuous angels covers the cinder blocks: their wings and breasts have absorbed the Clorox stink of the place. What prayer is in my book for him? The guard picks at his nail beds with his key. He says: "Two more minutes." My crucifix dangles from my chest like a fledgling.[7]

It seems that it is Reece's empathy that has led him into the priesthood, but religion is often insufficient to help the others he cares so deeply about.

Throughout the collection, in the course of autobiographical meditations, Reece engages issues surrounding homosexuality, referencing the Mesopotamian myth of Gilgamesh, a poem fragment by Sappho, and an apocryphal gospel. However, homosexuality is not, here, a subject that in itself necessitates much commentary. In fact, Reece at times seems eager to move away from—or to transcend—sexuality, as in "The Prodigal Son": "The soul has no sex and I am relieved / to speak of a thing alive in the world that has no sex."[8]

After the opening poem, the finest in *The Road to Emmaus* is the long prose poem "Hartford: Visions," a meditation on Reece's family history and his conflicted relationship with his mother. Lyricism returns full force here, along with a vatic voice enmeshed with the contemporary world, as Reece effectively incorporates Old Testament texts in such passages as the following:

> Long ago, missionaries tore down the sacred lodges of the Mohe-gans; now their casinos brighten the land like comic strips. *They have healed the wounds of my people lightly, saying: "Peace, peace," when there is no peace.*
>
> [...]
>
> *Why do you make me see wrongdoing and look at trouble?* A Puerto Rican mother weeps, her stabbed son intubated before us. Fluores-cence illuminates their pietá of pumps and wires.[9]

The central occasion for "Hartford: Visions" is a visit Reece and his mother make to a snowy cemetery, looking for the graves of their family members. Despite their past disagreements, Reece writes movingly of his mother, and their visit to the cemetery becomes a spiritual event:

7. Ibid., 103.

8. Ibid., 77.

9. Ibid., "Hartford: Visions," 86–87.

Passing beneath the sign "The Dead Shall Be Raised," erected upon faux-Egyptian granite columns, here is my mother, visiting the graves in their snowy ruins. Regard her, for she, like the city, was young once. "Do not say that I was beautiful once and now am old," the mother says to the poet, "Do not say that." And so the poem changes like the snow: the snow is white and black like the universe it came from. Hartford listens down the cemetery's long corridors. *How lonely sits the city that once was full of people.* Below the coffins are thick with facts like filing cabinets; some of the facts are correct, some misplaced, as the dead settle into their final category of aging, becoming a repository of mystery.[10]

The poet Wallace Stevens, who was a resident of Hartford, also haunts this poem. Stevens wrote, "The poet is the priest of the invisible." Reece writes, "A poet, like a priest, works with facts and mysteries: the facts mysterious, the mysteries factual."[11] And so it seems that, for Reece, poetry and the priesthood are two aspects of the same vocation. Both poetry and religion are explorations of mystery, and require a deep engagement with uncertainty. As Reece writes in two passages of "The Upper Room,"

I awaited what I could not see,
an activity that preoccupies many religious lives.[12]

and

We heard mice and bats in the walls gently tunneling;
they sounded like a hand holding a pen and writing
    in a diary,
moving forward with blind discovery.[13]

What makes Reece an effective poet is undoubtedly what makes him an effective priest: his desire to meet others in the darkness, awaiting what cannot be seen, and exploring alongside them the mystery of life.

10. Ibid., 86.

11. Ibid., 93.

12. Ibid., 118.

13. Ibid., 113.

An Auxiliar Light

Reciprocal Experience in *The Prelude*[1]

> *. . . An auxiliar light*
> *Came from my mind, which on the setting sun*
> *Bestowed new splendour . . . .*
>
> –Wordsworth, *The Prelude*[2] (II.369–371)

In *The Prelude*, an essential dichotomy is discernible in Wordsworth's view of the self: on one hand, there is the participatory tendency of the self, engaging with the natural world and with other selves; on the other hand, there is the egoistical self[3] that resists communion with the world or with others. This conflicted self—for it is indeed one self, though with diverging tendencies—is variously dominated by one tendency or the other. In fact, *The Prelude* is, in the largest scheme, the story of the eventual domination of the participatory self over the egoistical self in Wordsworth's life.

Wordsworth's project in *The Prelude* is, in addition to being an attempt to set forth a new poetic and linguistic technique, an autobiography of his mental and spiritual development, superficially akin to Rousseau's *Confessions*. The similarity of Wordsworth's and Rousseau's work was evident from the beginning; William Hazlitt writes, "We see no other difference between [Rousseau and Wordsworth] than that the one wrote in prose, the other in poetry."[4] Remarkably, this was written in 1816, and Hazlitt was, of course, ignorant of *The Prelude* (Hazlitt died in 1830, and *The Prelude* was published, except for a few brief excerpts, posthumously in 1850) and

---

1. N.B.: All references to *The Prelude* refer to the 1850 version, unless otherwise noted.

2. Wordsworth, *The Prelude*, 87.

3. Not to be conflated with Keats' term "egotistical sublime."

4. Hazlitt, 92.

was speaking of "the author of the *Lyrical Ballads*"[5] when he made this observation, an observation which was applicable, but is even more so regarding *The Prelude*.[6] These two projects are landmarks in the history of individualism, the progress of which J. H. Van den Berg traces from Augustine, to Luther and DaVinci, to Rousseau.[7] Joshua Wilner succinctly defines *individualism* as a view in which the individual "is ontologically prior to the identity and historical destiny of any larger collective entity [. . .] rather than determined as a derivative and subordinate part."[8] Protestantism, revolution, and autobiography are the major social and cultural phenomena that accompany the burgeoning sense of individualism that plays such a large part in Romantic literature and its successors (too numerous to list). Rousseau's *Confessions* and Wordsworth's *The Prelude* both demonstrate the preeminence of the individual as the locus of significance and as the moral and philosophical point of reference.

But why should Van den Berg cite (as is indeed typical) Rousseau as the embodiment of individualism, and not Wordsworth? Or why not cite Rousseau and Wordsworth in the same breath, so to speak? It is true that Rousseau's work is slightly earlier than Wordsworth's, but was *The Prelude* immediately influenced by the *Confessions*? W. J. T. Mitchell points out that "There is simply no direct evidence that Wordsworth ever read the *Confessions*," and notes that all of Wordsworth's references to Rousseau are to the "philosopher": "There is no doubt that Wordsworth read and was shaped by *The Social Contract* and *Emile*, but the place of the *Confessions* in his literary and psychological development remains uncertain."[9] Mitchell's argument does not lead to the conclusion that the *Confessions* was not an influence on Wordsworth, but that it was not necessarily a *model*. The influence of the *Confessions* was pervasive in society at the time, just as the influence of the seldom-read Darwin and Freud are pervasive today, and Wordsworth certainly did encounter the ideas of the *Confessions*, even if he never read it.

Though the concept of a psychological autobiography may have originated with Rousseau, Wordsworth's work is equally significant and innovative, largely because of its paradigmatic nature. Rousseau's individualism and Wordsworth's are almost diametrically opposed in this respect: the

5. Ibid., 92.

6. Mitchell, "Influence, Autobiography, and Literary History," 646.

7. Van den Berg, "The Subject and His [sic] Landscape," 58–62.

8. Wilner, "*I speak . . . ,*" 193.

9. Mitchell, 645.

most significant distinction between their projects is that Wordsworth's journey is intended to be a paradigm for his readers, for future generations; this stated intention contrasts with Rousseau's unequivocal claim to singularity. In this sense, one might go so far as to claim that Rousseau's *Confessions* does not truly champion the individual—it champions one individual, Rousseau, claiming his *singularity* (which is a distinct concept from *individualism*) and thus does not express individualism as a general philosophy—whereas Wordsworth's work champions and seeks to guide all individuals, asserting an essential *similarity*. Hazlitt was surely mistaken when he claimed that the only difference between the two writers was genre. No doubt Rousseau was an individualist, but Wordsworth was perhaps a "better" one—*The Prelude* certainly demonstrates individualism as a general view more adequately than does the *Confessions*. While Rousseau asserts his own individuality and uniqueness, Wordsworth asserts individuality for each person by demonstrating fundamental likenesses (the dual tendencies of the self) and shared experiences (the sublime), as well as by designing *The Prelude* as a guide for its readers. Wordsworth's paradigmatic intention for *The Prelude* will be revisited as we proceed.

Wordsworth had many ways of talking about the egoistical and participatory tendencies of the self; this essay hopes to trace noteworthy ones. Putting aside the question of influence, both Rousseau and Wordsworth viewed childhood experience as determinative of adulthood, thus it is proper that Wordsworth's discussion of the participatory self begin with his infancy. The most significant formative experience, in Wordsworth's view, is that of being in the arms of one's mother, which occupies much of his thought in the second book:

> . . . blest the Babe,
> Nursed in his Mother's arms, who sinks to sleep
> Rocked on his Mother's breast; who with his soul
> Drinks in the feelings of his Mother's eye!
> For him, in one dear Presence, there exists
> A virtue which irradiates and exalts
> Objects through widest intercourse of sense.[10]

If we are to trace the history of participation, this must be the first point we examine. Through physical and spiritual participation with the mother, the child receives love and a loving sensibility that result in an "intercourse of sense" that "irradiates and exalts objects," which is, in turn, an impartation

10. *The Prelude* (II.234–240), 79.

of love. This is the primal instance of the reciprocity Wordsworth speaks of again and again throughout *The Prelude*—an experience in which the individual both gives to nature and receives from it. Often, this takes the form of beautification ("irradiates and exalts objects"), as in the same passage continued from above, in which he describes a baby attempting to pick a flower:

> . . . already love
> Drawn from love's purest earthly fount for him
> Hath beautified that flower; already shades
> Of pity cast from inward tenderness
> Do fall around him . . . .[11]

It is important to note that this cycle of reciprocity begins by virtue of the mother's love, through participation with her. In the 1805 version, this idea is stated more plainly, when the child "claims manifest kindred with an earthly soul."[12] We must bear this aspect of Wordsworth's thought in mind when we examine the idea of sublimity—we do not want to make the mistake Harold Bloom makes when he says, "This sublimity, in its origins, has little to do with love or sympathy for others . . . ."[13] It is clear from the Mother passage that reciprocity must first occur between human souls before it can occur between the individual and the natural world, even if that sublime fellowship appears to be quite independent of other persons at the moment of its occurrence.

At this point, it is essential that we make certain to distinguish between Wordsworth's views as presented in *The Prelude* and his actual life and actions, which were, of course, not always entirely consistent with the ideas expressed in his work. The major philosophical and moral lapse of his life is not, as he would have it in *The Prelude*, his bout with rationalism, but rather his abandonment of Caroline, his daughter, and Annette, her mother. Given this fact, Bloom's statement about the "egotistical sublime" (to use Keats' pejorative term) perhaps seems more justified; however, our concern is not Wordsworth's biography, but his *autobiography*—that which he expresses in *The Prelude*. Regardless of Wordsworth's consistency (or lack thereof) with his stated philosophy, sublimity in *The Prelude* clearly has its origins in human love and fellowship, and leads to the same.

11. Ibid. (II.246–250), 79.

12. Ibid., 1805 version (II.242), 78.

13. Bloom, "Introduction," 9.

In the above passage, love, drawn from his mother, has been taken in and turned outward, beautifying the natural world. Wordsworth does not view nature as beautiful independent of the individual's participation with it—rather, it is that very participation which beautifies it:

> For feeling has to him imparted power
> That through the growing faculties of sense
> Doth like an agent of the one great Mind
> Create, creator and receiver both,
> Working but in alliance with the works
> Which it beholds.—Such, verily, is the first
> Poetic spirit of our human life,
> By uniform control of after years,
> In most, abated or suppressed; in some,
> Through every change of growth and of decay,
> Pre-eminent till death.[14]

Here, we see that nature joins the Mother in imparting the power by which it is beautified. As a child, the individual is "creator and receiver both," participating with and imitating God, "the one great Mind." This reciprocity, this participatory self, is "the first / Poetic spirit" which is "in most, abated or suppressed," but which remains for a happy few—Wordsworth, of course, figuring himself among them—"pre-eminent till death." Wordsworth is not claiming that the egoistical self never threatens to subdue the participatory self, as it indeed does later in his life, but that the participatory self is ultimately the victor. His plainly stated aim is to trace the growth and vigor of the "infant sensibility," referring to the "Poetic spirit" of line 261, which is what we have called the participatory self: "I have endeavoured to display the means / Whereby this infant sensibility, / Great birthright of our being, was in me / Augmented and sustained . . . ."[15]

The participatory self is the means of sublime experience, for sublimity is the immediate experience of participation—both frightening and fulfilling, both a giving up of the self and an assertion of the self, both a surrender and a triumph. "Fair seed-time had my soul, and I grew up / Fostered alike by beauty and by fear,"[16] declares Wordsworth, and this meeting of "discordant elements"[17] (as he calls them elsewhere) in a moment of

14. *The Prelude* (II.255–265), 79–80.
15. Ibid. (II.269–272), 81.
16. Ibid. (I.301–302), 45.
17. Ibid. (I.343), 47.

spiritual fellowship is the sublime itself. Perhaps it would be difficult to find a better metaphor than sex for the sublime experience; indeed, many of the sublime experiences related in *The Prelude* contain unmistakable sexual imagery. The early anecdote in which Wordsworth briefly steals a boat is a prime example. "It was an act of stealth / And troubled pleasure,"[18] he says, conveying immediately a sense of simultaneous guilt and enjoyment of the kind an adolescent boy might experience in a sexual situation:

> . . . lustily
> I dipped my oars into the silent lake,
> And as I rose upon the stroke my boat
> Went heaving through the water like a swan—
> When from behind that craggy steep, till then
> The bound of the horizon, a huge cliff,
> As if with voluntary power instinct,
> Upreared its head. I struck, and struck again,
> And, growing still in stature, the huge cliff
> Rose up between me and the stars, and still
> With measured motion, like a living thing
> Strode after me . . . .[19]

Though we certainly could spend much time on the sexual imagery and diction here, our purpose is only to point out the sexual comparison that seems implicit in the text of the sublime experience. The metaphor of sex is apt, for it describes a mutual act, a reciprocal encounter between the individual and nature. The boy has gone out to meet the natural world, taking a risk in a boat not his own, and his oar-strokes cause the cliff to grow and loom as it takes on a "voluntary power." Wordsworth celebrates his early troubling and joyous experiences, such as this one, with the sublime, declaring that the "Wisdom and Spirit of the universe" was

> purifying thus
> The elements of feeling and of thought,
> And sanctifying, by such discipline,
> Both pain and fear [. . .].
> Nor was this fellowship vouchsafed to me
> With stinted kindness.[20]

---

18. Ibid. (I.361–362), 49.

19. Ibid., 1805 version (I.401–412), 48 & 50.

20. Ibid. (I.410–416), 51.

Given Wordsworth's celebration of the sublime experience in nature, Bloom makes far too much of what he calls the "antagonism" of nature in relation to the individual. He says, for instance, that the reason for Wordsworth's crossing of the Alps "may be a desire to emancipate his maturing Imagination from Nature by overcoming the greatest natural barrier he can encounter."[21] In fact, Wordsworth's expedition in the Alps was a failed attempt (perhaps because it was an overly-conscious attempt) to *meet* nature, to join with it, rather than to be free of it—his disappointment at the end of the crossing is due not to having failed to conquer nature, but to having failed to sublimely experience it. Nowhere does Wordsworth seek to free his imagination from nature (unlike Blake, perhaps), for nature is and remains for him the source of the sublime imaginative power. To be more precise, nature is indeed antagonistic, but only to the egoistical tendency of the self; the sublime experience of the natural world is always a nurturing experience for the participatory self. Both in the above passage—in which nature's antagonism, if we must call it that, has a "purifying" and "sanctifying" effect—and in the following passage, we see that nature's antagonism is ultimately benevolent, that it fosters the participatory self:

> . . . How strange that all
> The terrors, pains, and early miseries,
> Regrets, vexations, lassitudes interfused
> Within my mind, should e'er have borne a part,
> And that a needful part, in making up
> The calm existence that is mine when I
> Am worthy of myself! Praise to the end!
> Thanks to the means which Nature deigned to
>   employ . . . .[22]

He goes on to praise even nature's "severer interventions,"[23] interventions, we must conclude, to combat the egoistical self and to foster the participatory self—that "calm existence" he experiences when he is "worthy of [him] self."

If nature fosters the participatory self, does urbanity antagonize it? One is tempted to say *yes*—virtually all of Wordsworth's sublime experiences occur in nature, away from the city. But one remembers as well a brief instance of sublimity when Wordsworth sees a beggar in the city, and

21. Bloom, 11–12.
22. *The Prelude* (I.344–351), 47 & 49.
23. Ibid. (I.355), 49.

then one thinks of his sonnets, which demonstrate subtlety in his views of the city and technology. In *The Prelude*, his view of urbanity is rather harsh:

> . . . now most thankful that my walk
> Was guarded from too early intercourse
> With the deformities of crowded life,
> And those ensuing laughters and contempts
> Self-pleasing, which, if we would wish to think
> With a due reverence on earth's rightful Lord,
> [. . .] Will not permit us . . . .[24]

The key phrase here is *self-pleasing*—"the deformities of crowded life" (what a strong distaste we sense here!) lead to self-pleasing vices. The designation *self-pleasing* is the key to understanding his thinking; city life threatens to foster the egoistical self, a self which, though surrounded by crowds, is ironically uninterested in a participatory relationship with others, and is therefore merely self-pleasing. Solitude, which typically implies for him a rural setting, apart from the "crowded life" of the city, is vital for the nurturing of the participatory self. Yet, we cannot quite claim that Wordsworth is altogether opposed to urbanity. Though too much of the city, too early, is detrimental in Wordsworth's view ("too early intercourse"), we never see him condemn urbanity outright. "The world is too much with us," he asserts in a sonnet written in his early thirties, "Little we see in Nature that is ours; / We have given our hearts away,"[25] yet, in "Steamboats, Viaducts, and Railways," a sonnet written in his sixties, he expresses faith that industrial advances will be assimilated into the natural world: "Nature doth embrace / Her lawful offspring in Man's art . . . ."[26] In *The Prelude*, Wordsworth's relationship with the city remains ambivalent, for urbanity carries with it the danger of feeding the self-pleasing, egoistical tendency.

If Wordsworth is wary of urbanity, he is not initially overly wary of politics, and sees it as an expression of the participatory self. During the height of his Revolutionary sympathies, he calls himself "An active partisan"[27] after making this metaphorical self-characterization:

24. Ibid. (VIII.330–337), 291.

25. Wordsworth, "[The world is too much with us]", lines 1–4, *The Norton* . . . , 297–298.

26. Wordsworth, "Steamboats, Viaducts, and Railways," lines 10–11, *The Norton* . . . , 299.

27. *The Prelude* (XI.153), 399.

> ... Earth was then
> To me, what an inheritance, new-fallen,
> Seems, when the first time visited, to one
> Who thither comes to find in it his home[.]
> He walks about and looks upon the spot
> With cordial transport, moulds it and remoulds ....[28]

This *moulding and remoulding* is the act of the participatory self, which not only engages transformatively with the natural world, but also with the political system, mutually giving and receiving, along with the other *active partisans*, the other participatory selves. This passage continues with a description of the congenial temperament that was his at that time, bearing even with political ideas contrary to his own. The participatory self has dominated at this point in his life, and has resulted in fellowship with many and patience with the rest—a love of others in general. He is quick to credit this to his childhood experience, calling himself "a child of Nature, as at first, / Diffusing only those affections wider / That from the cradle had grown up with me,"[29] a passage which recalls the Mother passage, in which he receives love from his mother, resulting in fellowship with nature.

This participatory condition is not yet perpetual; when England goes to war with France, Wordsworth says he was thrown "out of the pale of love."[30] This is the result of immaturity, not of any error in his former loving disposition: "a blow that, in maturer age, / Would but have touched the judgement, struck more deep / Into sensations near the heart ...."[31] The egoistical self here becomes dominant, as he attempts to prove his moral convictions by means of reason alone;[32] this is an exclusively inward turning (thus an egoistical tendency), a reliance upon his rational faculties alone, upon "Reason's naked self."[33] The ensuing psychological crisis is reversed only when his sister, Dorothy, comes to live with him. He remarks that she "Maintained for me a saving intercourse / With my true self,"[34] indicating his esteem of the

---

28. Ibid. (XI.145–150), 399.
29. Ibid. (XI.168–170), 399.
30. Ibid. (XI.176), 401.
31. Ibid. (XI.186–188), 401.
32. Ibid. (XI.279–305), 407.
33. Ibid. (XI.234), 403.
34. Ibid. (XI.341–342), 409.

participatory self and his abhorrence of the egoistical self, which had led him to despair.[35] He views Dorothy as an instrument of nature, which,

> By all varieties of human love
> Assisted, led me back through opening day
> To those sweet counsels between head and heart
> Whence grew that genuine knowledge, fraught
>   with peace,
> Which [. . .] / Hath still upheld me . . . .[36]

A healthy balance between rationality and sensibility is thus restored, and the participatory self begins to reclaim its status as the *true self.*

The nature of the balance between rationality and sensibility is not readily apparent in the phrase, "those sweet counsels between head and heart." He goes on in Book Twelfth to address nature ("ye Groves"), which intervenes to bring peace "between man himself [. . .] and his own uneasy heart."[37] We see here the self battling the self, Rationalism battling sensibility, the egoistical self battling the participatory self. In the 1805 version of Book Twelfth, Wordsworth opposes "self-applauding intellect" to "magnanimity";[38] Rationalism, then, is ultimately a selfish tendency, a reliance upon reason alone, without regard to the communications of nature or human love, as opposed to the participatory self, which results in "magnanimity." In the following passage, Wordsworth dramatizes the struggle between these two tendencies:

> In such strange passion [. . .]
> I warred against myself,
> [. . .] Like a cowled Monk who hath forsworn the world,
> Zealously laboured to cut off my heart
> From all the sources of her former strength . . . .[39]

We have here *sources* of his heart's former strength, so it is not adequate to mention nature alone. It is through the intervention of Dorothy, his sister, that he is restored. So, human fellowship is one of those sources of former strength, and it is the primary means of the restoration of the participatory

---

35. Ibid. (XI.305), 407.

36. Ibid. (XI.350–355), 409.

37. Ibid. (XII.27–28), 417.

38. Ibid. 1805 version (XII.31–32), 438.

39. Ibid. (XII.75–80), 421.

self. Just as fellowship with the mother is necessary for the primal development of the participatory self, continued fellowship with others is vital for its sustenance.

Now, if the participatory self implies a healthy balance of rationality and sensibility, a balance between "head and heart," how are these elements reconciled? Wordsworth's primary means of describing this reconciliation, resulting in what we have called the participatory self, is *imagination*. In the final book, Wordsworth describes the loving disposition of the participatory self:

> This spiritual Love acts not nor can exist
> Without Imagination, which, in truth,
> Is but another name for absolute power
> And clearest insight, amplitude of mind
> And Reason in her most exalted mood.
> This faculty hath been the feeding source
> Of our long labour . . . .[40]

Imagination is the human faculty that is open simultaneously to the communications of nature, the love of other human souls, and the intellect's reason. This is the animating force of his "long labor." Imagination results from the synthesis of reason and sensibility, and is the basis of the participatory self.

In Book Fourteenth, Wordsworth gives an allegory of the progress from egoistical self-absorption to participatory fellowship in the Mount Snowdon passage. As the three travelers climb the rough terrain, they are blinded by a fog, and are silent, lost in solitude and noncommunication. Solitude is rarely a negative idea for Wordsworth, but the kind of solitude that precludes human fellowship clearly is. They continue to climb, "as if in opposition set / Against an enemy,"[41] and gradually they rise above the fog. When they leave the fog behind, they see each other again and share an expansive view of the hills and sky and ocean. They do not speak to each other, but speech is not necessary for fellowship—sharing the experience is the fellowship itself. Wordsworth's vision of the participatory self is an ideal not only for himself, but for all individuals, whom he seeks to guide into sublime fellowship with nature and with each other.

We would be mistaken if we viewed Wordsworth's autobiography as merely that—an autobiography. He intended it as more than that. It is a

40. Ibid. (XIV.188–194), 469.
41. Ibid. (XIV.29–30), 459.

guide for all who struggle to overcome the egoistical tendency—those who are also climbing Mount Snowdon, those who yearn for sublime fellowship with nature and with others:

> . . . what we have loved,
> Others will love, and we will teach them how;
> Instruct them how the mind of man becomes
> A thousand times more beautiful than the earth
> On which he dwells . . . .[42]

The participatory self, begun in love and sustained by love, must necessarily result in love. It is not insignificant that *The Prelude* is addressed superficially to Wordsworth's beloved friend, Coleridge, and that he spent many nights reading his work aloud to Coleridge. Wordsworth intends not only *The Prelude* as a paradigm, but also the loving friendship it bears witness to and which is the immediate occasion of its composition. Wordsworth imagines (in *his* sense of the word) that others will find a way to more fully participate in the transformative reciprocity of sublime fellowship through his work. As a paradigm for others of the endurance and victory of the participatory self over the egoistical self, *The Prelude* enacts the very "love of man [sic]" which it describes, and demonstrates an individualistic philosophy quite distinct from the ego-centrism of Rousseau's *Confessions*.

42. Ibid. (XIV.448–452), 483.

II. Commentary & Personal Essays

On Virtuosity and Simplicity

When I was young, it seemed logical to me that the most virtuosic performances should be the "best" music, and most worthy of my appreciation. As my tastes ran more toward classic rock than classical music, I was particularly an advocate of Led Zeppelin's most fiery guitar and drum solos, or their more complex picking patterns in songs like "Babe, I'm Gonna Leave You" and "Black Mountain Side."

As I grew older I began to sense flaws in this way of thinking, as it privileged a proposition about music over the actual aesthetic experience of music. As I began to ponder this distinction, I noticed more and more how much I could be moved by the most simple of songs.

Don't get me wrong; I still love Led Zeppelin. But I now love realms of music that at one point seemed illogical for me to appreciate. The same is true of visual art and literature. I have grown into an attention to and profound love of the aesthetic experience of art, rather than allowing myself to be led by *a priori* notions of which forms the most powerful art "should" take. I believe that only after experiencing a work of art should one attempt to identify the objective features that create the possibility of a powerful aesthetic experience. In this way, the aesthetic experience is neither entirely subjective nor entirely objective, but subjectivity and objectivity coexist—indeed, must coexist—in the aesthetic experience.

In his essay, "Play and Theory of the Duende," Federico García Lorca examines the mysterious quality in art (for him, most particularly in dance, music, and poetry) that lends it power to transport an audience. He calls this *duende*, a dark force of the earth, something other than the "muse" or the "angel," rising from the mortal center of the artist rather than arriving from without. Lorca gives an example of an old flamenco dancer at a competition:

> Years ago, an eighty-year-old woman won first prize at a dance contest in Jerez de la Frontera. She was competing against beautiful women and young girls with waists supple as water, but all she

did was raise her arms, throw back her head, and stamp her foot on the floor. In that gathering of muses and angels—beautiful forms and beautiful smiles—who could have won but for her moribund duende, sweeping the ground with its wings of rusty knives.[1]

She gives an utterly simple, unadorned performance—hardly even worthy to be called a dance. But her performance is so impassioned, so full of the acknowledgment of death, so full of *duende*, that she is transported by her dance, sweeping up the audience along with her, and is awarded first prize over all the ornate performances of her young and beautiful competitors. This is part of what I'm getting at when I talk about the experience of a work of art. The superficial features one might expect beforehand to produce a powerful aesthetic experience are not reliably the ones that actually do produce the greatest effect. It is not perfect execution or virtuosity that is the most profound aspect of art, but rather its ability to evoke the heart of the human condition, to allow us to transcend the bounds of time and mortality for a moment through the unwavering insistence on those limits. This is a mysterious power that we can experience in two arenas: art and spirituality. At heart, I suspect that these two practices are, or can be, one and the same.

This mortal passion that takes simple artistic forms has an amazing ability to endure, to retain its power to move the reader or viewer or listener, no matter how many times the work of art is revisited. This is not to say that virtuosic art or more traditionally "beautiful" art doesn't have this same power—think of Keats' Grecian urn: "When old age shall this generation waste, / Thou shalt remain, in midst of other woe / Than ours, a friend to man . . . "[2] —but it is suprising to speak of simple art this way because it seems counterintuitive to think that utter simplicity should remain powerful over time. The simple, unadorned poem or song is the most easily remembered, but because of its simplicity we might assume that its aesthetic effect would diminish over time, while more complex art would offer new layers of meaning and beauty to the searching subject. But often expressions of the most fundamental aspects of the human condition depend for their effect not on elaboration or adornment, but the opposite.

This is why, in the visual arts, I've grown to love Mark Rothko, whose best work is minimalistic, and yet strikes the viewer as *perfect* in the sense of being complete, final. In music, the Estonian composer Arvo Pärt is a particular favorite of mine. For the same reasons, much Eastern poetry is among the work I most cherish. In the space of a handful of syllables, a

1. Lorca, 54.
2. Keats, *Complete Poems* . . . , 239–240.

poem can resonate as deeply as—dare I say it?—an epic poem by Dante or Milton. Buson writes:

> The moth alights
> on the one-ton temple bell.[3]

Issa writes:

> On a branch
> floating downriver,
> a cricket, singing.[4]

Li Po writes:

> The birds have vanished down the sky.
> Now the last cloud drains away.
> We sit together, the mountain and I,
> until only the mountain remains.[5]

Rumi writes:

> We are the mirror as well as the face in it.
> We are tasting the taste this minute
> of eternity. We are pain
> and what cures pain, both. We are
> the sweet cold water and the jar that pours.[6]

The *Tao te Ching*, in Stephen Mitchell's sublime translation, reads:

> Yet mystery and manifestations
> arise from the same source.
> This source is called darkness.
>
> Darkness within darkness.
> The gateway to all understanding.[7]

Simplicity: a door opening on the depths, a rung toward the heavens.

---

3. I wrote down this translation some years ago, but unfortunately failed to note the translator, whom I have been unable to locate, despite a thorough search of books and the Web. This is the best version of Buson's haiku I've encountered, free of embellishment as it is. My apologies to the translator for this oversight, which I hope to correct in a future edition, if possible.

4. Issa (no page number).

5. Po, "Zazen on Ching-t'ing Mountain," (no page number).

6. Rumi, 106.

7. Lao-tzu, 1.

A Way of Happening

Some Thoughts on "Art for Art's Sake"

Frequently, people quote the portion of W. H. Auden's poem "In Memory of W. B. Yeats" that says "poetry makes nothing happen," but ignore completely the positive assertion he makes about poetry at the end of that stanza (in the same sentence, in fact) when he calls poetry "a way of happening." This is not a diminishment of art, but a valorization of it and a clarification of its most basic function. It makes nothing happen, perhaps, but it is itself a way of happening. Here is section II in its entirety:

> You were silly like us; your gift survived it all:
> The parish of rich women, physical decay,
> Yourself. Mad Ireland hurt you into poetry.
> Now Ireland has her madness and her weather still,
> For poetry makes nothing happen: it survives
> In the valley of its making where executives
> Would never want to tamper, flows on south
> From ranches of isolation and the busy griefs,
> Raw towns that we believe and die in; it survives,
> A way of happening, a mouth.[1]

The 19th-century idea of "art for art's sake" has become not only a cliché, but a joke in common usage, eliciting rolling eyes or smug chuckles whenever the phrase is heard. This is unfortunate, because it means that we, in general, have stopped considering the implications of adopting the alternate view that art must necessarily serve some "outside" purpose. Auden, in his elegy for Yeats, is espousing precisely the "art for art's sake" view, which is worth expounding: "Art for art's sake" means, for instance, that a poem is valuable as an end in itself, rather than merely as a means toward some other, utilitarian end. If a work of art is viewed as purely causal—that is,

---

1. Auden, 248.

if its value is predicated on its effecting additional, exterior, tangible phe-nomena—then it means that we have forgotten that the work of art is itself an effect. This is more than an argument over semantics. A poem (Auden's elegy for Yeats, for instance) is valuable already, in itself, as a work of art. If it causes no additional effects, it is still valuable as an effect that we, as readers, can experience firsthand. Another way of putting it is to say that the poem is valuable as an aesthetic work and a record of ideas—as some-thing that can be experienced for its own sake, rather than for the sake of any pragmatic function it may (or may not) serve. That is not to preclude the idea that art can have pragmatic function; but I would caution against locating art's primary value in pragmatism, at least insofar as "pragmatism" implies tangible effects on the so-called "outside world" (politics, society, etc.).

If poetry (and art in general) is "a way of happening," then we can value a work of art for the very experience of engaging with the work. Art is an effect to be experienced rather than a cause to be tested for its utilitarian impact on the world at large. The happy irony is, if we view and engage with art in this way it is far more likely to have a tangible effect on the levels of society and poli-tics. However, we should never look to those effects as the primary source of art's value.

Art in a Time of War

What is the function of art in a time of war? is a perennial question among artists. Art has historically served both the propagandistic purposes of the state as well as the protestations of dissenters. Much of this art, of course, has been and continues to be overtly "political." We are in an age in America in which it seems that, when they do produce overtly "political" work, artists rarely produce work favorable to the wars of the state. It's not a popular stance among literary types, to say the least.

In my mind, it is completely appropriate for artists to be aligned against the purposes of war, and I would argue that, generally speaking, this stance is faithful to the age-old function of art.

The state's message in a time of war is a message of dichotomy. The language and images of the state, the military, and the media are focused on differentiating the enemy from us. It is the state's goal to subtly convince the public of essential dissimilarity between us and them.

Consider the ever-present lauding of "democracy" in American political speech in times of war and "military action." Politicians speak of democracy as a good in and of itself, in an attempt to justify the imposition of it on other nations, as if democratic nations had never committed atrocities of their own (e.g., the U.S. fire bombings and nuclear bombings in Japan, which targeted civilian children, women, and men, killing between 500,000 and 1,000,000 civilians).

The tactic of the state, the military, and the media in general is to present us with simplistic, easy-to-believe lies about ourselves and about the other. These lies boil down to plain dichotomies: *We are virtuous. The enemy is evil. We are reasonable. The enemy is unreasonable. We have a superior political system. The enemy's political system is fundamentally flawed.*

The artist, on the other hand, most often does the opposite—that is, the artist bears witness to the essential similarity between one human and another, and by extension, between all humans. Joseph Conrad beautifully expressed this idea in his famous "Preface":

> [The artist] speaks to our capacity for delight and wonder, to the sense of mystery surrounding our lives; to our sense of pity, and beauty, and pain; to the latent feeling of fellowship with all creation—and to the subtle but invincible conviction of solidarity that knits together the loneliness of innumerable hearts: to the solidarity in dreams, in joy, in sorrow, in aspirations, in illusions, in hope, in fear, which binds men to each other, which binds together all humanity—the dead to the living and the living to the unborn.[1]

While the state, the military, and the media are engaged in oversimplification, the artist is engaged in complexities. Again, here is Conrad:

> [A]rt itself may be defined as a single-minded attempt to render the highest kind of justice to the visible universe, by bringing to light the truth, manifold and one, underlying its every aspect. It is an attempt to find in its forms, in its colours, in its light, in its shadows, in the aspects of matter and in the facts of life, what of each is fundamental, what is enduring and essential—their one illuminating and convincing quality—the very truth of their existence. [. . .] [T]he artist descends within himself [sic], and in that lonely region of stress and strife, if he be deserving and fortunate, he finds the terms of his appeal. His appeal is made to our less obvious capacities: to that part of our nature which, because of the warlike conditions of existence, is necessarily kept out of sight within the more resisting and hard qualities—like the vulnerable body within the steel armour.[2]

It is noteworthy that Conrad describes those conditions that suppress our "less obvious capacities"—that is, our more humane, empathetic nature—as "warlike." The implication is that war is the ultimate suppressor of these underlying humane capacities, and that art is a force that attempts to counteract the "warlike" aspects of life. In fulfilling this vision of art's function, the artist need not write overtly about political matters, the war(s) at hand, or even the "warlike conditions of existence." It is the empathy itself and the acknowledgment of both fundamental similarity and unsoundable

1. Conrad, 120.
2. Ibid.

complexity of the other expressed in the artist's work that performs this function, regardless of subject or setting.

W. B. Yeats, in his poem "On Being Asked for a War Poem," seems to disparage the idea of writing a poem about war:

> I think it better that in times like these
> A poet's mouth be silent, for in truth
> We have no gift to set a statesman right;
> He has had enough of meddling who can please
> A young girl in the indolence of her youth,
> Or an old man upon a winter's night.[3]

The possibility that Yeats seems to have overlooked in this response, however, is the possibility that a work of art need not overtly address the policies or programs or statements of the state—instead, pleasing that young girl or that old man through a work of art might itself be the function that counteracts the machinations of the state and "set[s] a statesman right."

---

3. Yeats, 155–156.

A Piece of Advice

When you've written yourself into a corner, don't throw the draft away—not yet, not in the first flush of frustration. Sometimes the repair the essay or poem or story needs can only occur to you out of the action of the subconscious, which can only take place with time. Where you see no way out of the mess you've made of things, a lovely little path through the detritus might come clear in a day, a week, a year, pulling all the scattered elements together as bricks to be laid down beneath the reader's feet.

Some Thoughts on Value in Art

I once saw a blank white canvas—not even painted with white paint—bolted to the wall at Le Centre Pompidou in Paris. There was a placard next to the canvas with a title and name of the "artist" (though I've forgotten the names). I thought at the time, and still do, that this canvas had no place in a museum. An idea does not automatically qualify as art.

Robert Rauschenberg famously made a series of monochromatic paintings (I don't believe it was a Rauschenberg that was on display at Pompidou; for one, there was no paint on that canvas, and Rauschenberg used paint even on his white paintings). John Cage, speaking about Rauschenberg's white canvases, called them "airports of the lights, shadows, and particles."[1] (This is not at all surprising, coming from the famous "composer" of the silent "4'33"—which came, by the way, as Cage himself pointed out, after Rauschenberg's monochromes.) My response to that notion would be that the wall of the nearest building, the floor, and a leaf (three instances out of innumerable ones) are equally "airports of the lights, shadows, and particles." I find Cage's attempt at discerning value or craft in the blank canvas unconvincing.

Some would argue (and many do) that this work has to be considered in the context of the "conversation" of which it was a part. I'm dubious about the status as art of any artwork that depends for its effect on its audience being part of a meta-level "conversation" about art or the work's particular genre. Those works seem to me less artful than political, foregrounding the "meaning" or "statement" and minimizing the aesthetic effect of experiencing the work. I'm not opposed to education or understanding of the context in which art arises and works within and reacts against, of course. But if scholarship or entrée is the *only* means by which to appreciate a work of art, its worth is severely limited. Education about the context can enrich the experience (think of the way this might happen for someone reading a

1. Cage, 102.

19th-century novel, for instance), but if that kind of knowledge offers the only richness to be had in experiencing the work, then I would say that the work doesn't function as art at all, but rather as a political billboard or a social commentary or philosophical proposition. This is not to say that art should not be "political" or "philosophical" or be engaged in a historically located conversation. Rather, what I mean is that when the message (and even an apparent utter lack of a message constitutes a message because it tells us about the artist's ideas about art, if about nothing else)—when the message supersedes the experience of the medium in importance for the artist and, by extension, for the viewers, then I think it would be strange to call such a work "art." It's become more like an essay than a poem, more like a lecture than a drama, more like a billboard than a canvas.

I also think it's important to consider what we value, how much we value it, and why. If Rauschenberg's monochromatic canvases are a reaction against other artists or philosophies of art, then ok, it's a "statement." A "statement" (act of communication) might be considered art. Even so, I'd relegate a work that is purely, or at least primarily, a "statement" about art rather than a rich aesthetic experience in itself to the less valuable end of the artistic spectrum. (Sure, you can experience a statement, but it's a weak experience compared to other artistic experiences.) In my view, art should have itself, rather than any "conversation," as its primary and most essential source of power, of having an effect on the viewer. Museums and public places and literary journals and publishing houses ought to champion and preserve those works of art that are most worthy of our giving them value— i.e., those that offer the richest and most significant experiences to those who value them.

There is also the opposite problem, namely, "art" that attempts to divorce the aesthetic from any intentionality—indeed, from any work—by the so-called artist or writer. A good example of this is poetry that is entirely computer-generated. Reading a computer-generated poem may be an aesthetic experience, but such a poem does not qualify as art because there is no craftsmanship by a conscious mind. Art is a shaping, a primarily aesthetic intentionality in a tangible medium. Blank canvases and computer-generated poems are not art because they either lack the primacy of the aesthetic, no matter how much work went into them, or lack intentionality (i.e., work, shaping, craft) despite any aesthetic effect they may have. This has what seem to me clear implications for value.

Much of this already sounds like a manifesto. Here's an attempt at one:

A Manifesto on Art

Part 1

1. Manifestos are inevitably imperfect and insufficient, but they can be a means of articulating ideas and fostering discussion.

2. Art is artifice. It is a made thing. (This idea is inherent in the etymology of English words: *poem* comes from the Greek verb that means "to make"; *art* originated in the Latin word for "craftsmanship"; *artifice* comes the Latin word for "skill.") Thus, art is inherently *creative* in the literal sense of that word.

3. Given (2), in order to be considered a work of art, some amount of actual work has to have been done, some action taken on the medium.

4. Given (3), something that expresses an idea (or makes a "statement") does not necessarily qualify as art. A blank canvas or blank sheet of paper would not qualify. (Another of Rauschenberg's works, "Erased de Kooning Drawing," for example, would barely qualify, in my view. The blankness, in this case, is the result of work, however, so I wouldn't say it's absolutely not art. [In fact, a lot of work went into it, by Rauschenberg's account, because de Kooning purposely gave him something that would be difficult to erase, a page that had charcoal and paint and crayon.] Works of that nature function primarily on the level of meta-art, and are thus more expository than what I would call creative. "Erased de Kooning" seems to be primarily a "statement" rather than a creation—or an attempt to create a cause rather than an effect. No matter how much work went into it, I would argue that it is the idea of what he did that is significant rather than the product itself, thus this work does not function primarily as an aesthetic experience, but as a representation of an idea. This is at the lowest end of the spectrum of art, in my view, hardly deserving the label. An example of something that, in my schema, is decidedly not art would be John Cage's "4'33" [mentioned above], a "composition" consisting entirely of three movements of silence. Note that this might, indeed, qualify as a "statement," but not as a work of art, not as a made thing—as it is neither made nor a thing.)

Part 2

1. Value, as regards a work of art (see Part 1), is a measure of the potential reward of engagement (by a person) inherent in that work. Note that the potential is inherent in the work of art, given its physical properties, but not the value itself. Value is primarily an action (on the part of the valuer) rather than a characteristic of the work itself—it is a function of a complex interaction between the human experiencer and the work being experienced.

2. Works of art reward individuals in different ways and at different levels, but the potential reward should be thought of as the sum total of the amounts of reward experienced by a representative audience. (An assumption underlying this claim is that both subjectivity and objectivity exist simultaneously—and, in fact, are interdependent. We have subjective responses to an objective reality [an object or thing that is actual—that exists independent of our perceiving it].)

3. Some works of art are more worthy of value (i.e., reward valuation more highly) than other works of art. (Upon reflection, you will likely see that this claim does not contradict [2] above.)

4. Something can be art without being good art; i.e., the term *art* is not a statement of value, but art is the subject of valuation. The term *art* is a statement of process (see Part 1).

The *Paris Review* Poetry Purge

Some Ethical & Professional Considerations

When Daniel Nester broke the story of what he termed "The Great *Paris Review* Poetry Purge of 2010" on the blog We Who Are About To Die in July of this year,[1] a flurry of online discussion quickly followed. Lorin Stein and Robyn Creswell had recently been instated as Editor and Poetry Editor, respectively, of the *Paris Review*, and shortly thereafter they "de-accepted" poems that had been accepted for publication by previous editors. A wide range of opinions regarding this de-acceptance was expressed in online forums, predominantly on blogs, but also in such venues as the *New York Observer* and Canada's *National Post*. The responses ranged from basically saying "Tough luck" to calling for punitive measures against the editors.

Renewing the zeal of commenters was the eventual revelation that this poetry purge was in fact not the first event of its kind in the history of *TPR*. A number of poets have reported that they had their poems "purged" in 2005, including Joel Brouwer (again, see Daniel Nester's coverage, which includes interviews with several de-accepted poets—or "Purgerati," as they have come to be known) and my friend and colleague Keith Flynn. What's even more surprising, perhaps, is the fact that Robyn Creswell himself was a victim of the previous purge. Stein indicated the following to me[2]: "Robyn—when he used to write poems—had one accepted by Richard Howard and killed when Richard was fired. We both laughed it off at the time as a bit of bad luck. [. . .] I do understand that others would see it as an injustice—but it simply didn't occur to either of us back then."

Lorin Stein's justification for "killing" previously accepted poems in the most recent purge was "to give Robyn [Creswell] the scope to define

---

1. This article originally appeared in *The Writer's Chronicle* in 2010.

2. Permission from the correspondents has been obtained for all quotes from private correspondence in this article.

his own section," as he put it in his de-acceptance e-mail to the Purgerati (reproduced in one of Nester's articles). Another complicating factor became clear over time: Stein and Creswell were facing a large backlog of accepted poems (roughly a year's worth), so that the influence of the newly appointed Poetry Editor would not have been felt for quite some time if they had published them all. Some online commenters saw this fact alone as justification for the "purge," and preferred to lay blame on the previous editors who had built up such a sizeable backlog. Others pointed out that there was no signed contract with any of the Purgerati, in any case, and thus no legal obligation to publish the poems. Still others noted that a "kill fee" is sometimes offered for pieces that are cut from newspapers or magazines, and suggested that such a fee would have been a more appropriate way for Stein to handle the situation.

I think, however, that there is a more fundamental ethical issue involved in this situation that none of the above perspectives address. The most basic assumption underlying my perspective on the ethics of the poetry purges is that an editor is not commensurate with the publication he or she represents. An editor (and, by extension, an entire editorial staff) is a representative of a larger entity, in a position of service to a purpose that extends beyond the person or persons acting in editorial capacity. In the case of a continuous publication (i.e., a publication with a history and, theoretically, a future as the "same" publication, under the same name), while an editor does and should exercise control over the content of the publication, he or she should also honor any commitments that the publication as an institution has already made. The implications of such a view have obvious relevance to the most recent poetry purge: The poems that Stein de-accepted had already been accepted not by any individual as merely an individual, but by a person representing *TPR* as an entity. Thus, *TPR* remains obligated to publish the work that has been accepted even by previous editors.

As a result of my stance, I created a "group" on the social networking website Facebook that I called "Conditional Boycott of the *Paris Review*." I outlined my views regarding the poetry purge and the conditions of the boycott in the group's description. The group was never large—there are currently fifty-two members—and includes a former *TPR* Poetry Editor (currently an Advisory Editor), at least one past *TPR* contributor, and several other prominent poets and editors. I created the group on principle, with little hope that it would even be noticed by the folks at *TPR*. However, the group did end up playing a part, along with many other sources of protest and debate, both private and public, in attracting the attention of Stein and convincing him to make amends with the writers he had treated poorly.

I wrote a private message to Stein outlining the group's position. That message read in part: "The 'de-accepted' writers had contractual [agreements] (verbal contracts should be honored in a just society) with the *Paris Review*, not with any individual. Your current editorial position is actually irrelevant to the fact that their poems were accepted by previous editors *on behalf of* the *Paris Review*." I also invited Stein to join the group himself in order to engage in discussion. To his credit, he did join, and he responded to my message and to the group's stance publicly on the group's "wall" and "discussion board." He said, in part, "I have to say, I agree with you entirely. I feel a strong duty, as the new editor of the *Review*, to shape the magazine as best I can, according to the lights of our new staff. But having heard powerful arguments from several of the poets whose work we cut (and having read the posts of Daniel Nester's blog), I'm also persuaded that we have a lasting obligation to every poet whose work was accepted by the editors who came before us. I'm about to write to these poets personally, to express my apologies and to offer the full fee that we owe them."

As it turned out, Stein offered more than he at first indicated he would. Nester reported from primary sources on his blog that Stein offered not only an apology and the full fee owed the poets, but also publication on The *Paris Review* Daily, the magazine's blog, with an introduction for each poet by one of the former Poetry Editors (now Advisory Editors), Meghan O'Rourke or Dan Chiasson. As a result of this news, after consulting with the members of the boycott group, I officially ended the boycott (though the group still exists as a forum for discussion and as an archive). Stein's engagement with the boycott group and response to the Purgerati is admirable, especially considering the small size of the boycott group, which, in all honesty, did not pose a real threat as a boycott.

In personal correspondence, both Meghan O'Rourke and Dan Chiasson expressed to me their appreciation for the efforts of the literary community to convince Stein and Creswell to make amends with the Purgerati. "I'm glad you did this [created the boycott group], and glad it seems to have made a difference," Chiasson said. "As you can see," he added, "Lorin's a good guy, great mind, great skill and unprecedented gift as an editor, amazing energy for the paper; I just disagreed with his decision about poetry." It's clear that O'Rourke and Chiasson both disagreed with Stein's decision to de-accept poems (see Nester's coverage for a statement by O'Rourke), and they undoubtedly played a role in his eventual decision to seek to make amends. It seems clear that, thanks to the literary community, including his friends, his colleagues, online reporters and commenters, and the boycott group, Stein came to be genuinely convinced about the unethical nature of his decision. Writing to me, Stein said, "I've learned a bunch of lessons from the last week. Your very well-reasoned letter was the final clarification for me. All of which is to say, thanks." Stein's willingness to apologize, to make amends with the Purgerati, and his expressions of gratitude toward those of us who protested his decision all seem to demonstrate that Stein recognizes that his action was a mistake and genuinely intends to behave fairly.

The most important aspect of the *TPR* poetry purges is the fact that they have raised ethical and professional issues relevant to editorial practice at literary publications. This is a rather isolated practice in the world of literary publications. But the fact that such an event has happened at least twice at *TPR* alone, not to mention any unreported instances there or elsewhere, is good enough reason to carefully consider the ethical and professional implications for editorial practice.

In a post on the boycott group's discussion board, Keith Flynn shared some of his thoughts on the ethical issues involved in the poetry purges. He wrote that he joined the boycott group and offered his opinions "not because I have been treated shabbily by the *Paris Review*, but because as editors we have a personal responsibility as caretakers of the journals we create to treat with tenderness all the folks who trust us to comment upon, to judge, and support their hard-won efforts in the small but immense minority that is the poetry community." Regarding the de-acceptance of his poem in 2005, Flynn remarked, "In my thirty-year career as a poet, musician, and editor, this is the only time this has happened to me . . . . [W]e as editors have a particularly poignant mission to treat every submitted work with the same respect as we hope to receive when other editors contemplate our own carefully constructed poems. It is basic human fairness, but sometimes it is all we have."

Calling it an issue of fairness may be the best way to describe what is, ultimately, a very simple ethical issue. So many literary publications today operate entirely on a good-faith basis that it has become a standard practice—a kind of "honor system" that no one expects to be broken. This is evidence that editors in general have agreed that they, as editors, have a good-faith obligation to honor even verbal contracts because, as Flynn noted, "It is basic human fairness." In other words, we operate this way not because we are forced to by law or by any outside agent, but because we wouldn't dream of treating people unfairly—and we have faith that others will behave likewise.

In cases in which an instinct for fairness does not prove sufficient, such as the most recent "poetry purge," I would emphasize the principle that I have suggested above: An editor is not commensurate with his or her publication, and acts as a representative of a larger entity with a life that extends both before and after the editor's tenure. Thus, it makes sense to think of the publication itself as engaging in certain obligations. These obligations might indeed prove impossible to fulfill for financial or practical reasons, but that is not the case with the "poetry purge" at *TPR*. This was simply an instance of a difference of opinion about the merits of certain poems. For the sake of their aesthetic opinions, Stein and Creswell were willing to break the obligation of *TPR* to the poets whose work had been accepted by previous editors. In my mind, this is not sufficient reason to break an obligation, as Stein himself seems to have admitted.

It is interesting that so many literary publications these days subscribe to a set of written ethical guidelines for any contests they hold, and yet few, if any, have thought it necessary to instate written ethical guidelines for their general, everyday editorial practices. (Some publications make brief remarks about "considering each submission carefully," but that is typically the extent of it.) The reason for this is most likely the fact that, as noted above, the "honor system" has worked most of the time for many years. The popularity of written ethical guidelines for literary contests is due in large part to the exposure over the years of certain questionable or outright unethical practices on the part of contest judges (e.g., awarding prizes to friends or former students). It will be interesting to see if a similar phenomenon takes place in response to the poetry purges at *TPR*. Perhaps more literary publications will begin using written contracts for each poem (or prose piece) accepted. Perhaps many will continue to operate on the "honor system," which has worked perfectly well in the majority of cases. Still others might find it advisable to adopt written ethical guidelines in order to be transparent about their professional practice, which is standard practice in a number of other professional fields. This last measure, in any case, could easily be implemented by any publication, regardless of whether they use written contracts. What is certain is that the best way to maintain respect as a literary publication is to behave fairly at all times, and editors would do well to invest time in considering, developing, and articulating their views of what it means to do so.

Beautiful Truths?

Reason and Fundamentalist Christianity

with the threat of hell hanging over my head like a halo
i was made to believe in a couple of beautiful truths

–David Bazan, "When We Fell"[1]

Ask questions long enough about the theology of fundamentalist Christians and you inevitably reach a point at which you are advised to "suspend"
your reason. Having grown up in a fundamentalist Christian culture—specifically, in the Presbyterian Church in America, a very conservative branch
of the Calvinist, Protestant tradition—this happened to me time and again
over the course of my adolescence and early adulthood. (I left the church
at age 25.) Fundamentalist Christians believe that the Bible is perfectly and
literally true, at least in its original languages, though some of the smaller
and least intellectual fundamentalist sects also assert this of the Authorized
(i.e., "King James") Version. Fundamentalists believe that the composition
of scripture was overseen by God ("God-breathed," as the New Testament
puts it[2]). A literal interpretation and application of the words of scripture
is the only acknowledged authority for a fundamentalist, and it supersedes
any other consideration—including the operations of reason.

---

1. "When We Fell" and "In Stitches," lyrics from the album *Curse Your Branches*, ©
2009 David Bazan, used by permission of David Bazan. Formatting has been retained as
it appears on www.davidbazan.com (including lack of capitalization and punctuation).

2. An irony is that perhaps the most common reason cited by fundamentalists for believing the Bible to be infallible is the Bible's own assertion
(2 Timothy 3:16) that scripture is "God-breathed." (Of course, the author meant the Old
Testament, but this characteristic is ascribed by fundamentalists to both Old and New
Testaments.) I was presented with this biblical passage as evidence for the Bible's infallibility throughout my upbringing, both in church and at the Christian schools I attended.

If one's goal is to arrive as expeditiously as possible to this point of suspended rationality in conversation with a fundamentalist Christian, I can advise which are the most efficient avenues of inquiry: the infallibility of scripture, The Fall and the doctrine of original sin, hell and God's justice, and human free will coupled with God's foreknowledge will all lead any decent analytical thinker into territory where she is either explicitly asked by a fundamentalist to suspend the faculty of reason, or is simply presented with arguments that do not stand up to rational analysis.

David Bazan, a musician who likewise was raised in a fundamentalist Christian culture and left it in early adulthood, has written many songs that efficiently and piercingly express the dilemmas and dead ends he has encountered in fundamentalist theology. Consider his song "When We Fell," which addresses the Genesis narratives of Creation and The Fall, and the New Testament interpretations of these:

> with the threat of hell hanging over my head like a halo
> i was made to believe in a couple of beautiful truths
> that eventually had the effect of completely unraveling
> the powerful curse put on me by you
>
> when you set the table and when you chose the scale
> did you write a riddle that you knew they would fail
> did you make them tremble so they would tell the tale
> did you push us when we fell
>
> if my mother cries when i tell her what i have discovered
> then i hope she remembers she taught me to follow my heart
> and if you bully her like you've done me with fear of damnation
> then i hope she can see you for what you are
>
> what am i afraid of, whom did i betray
> in what medieval kingdom does justice work this way
> if you knew what would happen and made us just the same
> then you, my lord, can take the blame

The problem of a Creator who makes creatures who are fallible; presents them with a situation in which, by virtue (pun intended) of one mistake, they can doom not only their own souls but those of all humanity; and knew all along that they would make this mistake is an insurmountable obstacle to believing in the goodness of the Creator. Traditional Christian theology would assert here (a) that scripture (remember, believed to be literally overseen by God and therefore infallible) teaches that God is good, and therefore it is a fact that cannot be called into question, regardless of our opinion of the actions ascribed to God in the same scriptures, and (b) that the concept of "goodness" cannot be conceived outside of God in the first place, and therefore is not an exterior paradigm to be applied to God's nature; rather, God's nature itself is the definition of "goodness." I have encountered both of these arguments innumerable times in my conversations growing up as a Christian. I will address these two claims in order.

Apart from lacking evidence for the belief, the primary misstep fundamentalists make in asserting the infallibility of scripture occurs when historical or logical inconsistencies are encountered in scripture, and the assumption of infallibility is called upon as a basis for discounting human reason—not to mention textual and historical scholarship, that product of reason. The logic goes like this: *If the Bible is infallible and perfectly true, then we must believe everything it says; therefore, if it says something that seems contradictory to my reason, reason itself must be at fault, and scripture remains infallible.* So, even if based on a false starting assumption, the faculty of reason is used to conclude in the face of insurmountable logical contradictions that the faculty of reason itself is flawed and unreliable.

But how can one use reason to conclude that reason itself is untrustworthy? If reason truly is unreliable, then reason cannot be relied upon to inform you of this fact.[3] Fundamentalism is a state in which a belief is adhered to not merely in the absence of positive evidence, but in the presence of negative evidence.[4] When reason tells a fundamentalist that a belief is untenable, she nevertheless maintains the belief, whereas a non-fundamentalist would admit that the belief needed to be adjusted or reconsidered altogether. For a fundamentalist, changing a core belief is not an option. I think—and my personal experience confirms—that sociological and psychological influences are the primary forces causing fundamentalists

3. The arguments of secular philosophers who assert the unreliability of reason are equally tautological. The faculty of reason cannot be used to reach the conclusion that the faculty of reason is unreliable. This is the height of absurdity. It's like swimming out to a drowning person and yelling back to shore that you've discovered conclusive evidence that humans are unable to swim. By contrast, the reliability of reason can be (and I believe *is*) confirmed by something outside itself—experience. Thus, the person watching the swimmer from the shore reliably concludes that humans are indeed able to swim.

4. The philosopher Alvin Plantinga has done interesting work in support of the reasonability of theism, considering a lack of *defeaters*, although the arguments do little, if anything, to support fundamentalist theology (apart from the broad characteristic of theism). See especially *Warranted Christian Belief* (Oxford University Press, 2000).

to maintain their core beliefs. Growing up in a fundamentalist Christian subculture, all the people around you, from the cradle—your family, your church group, oftentimes your schoolmates and other friends—hold tenaciously to a core set of beliefs. And there is also "the threat of hell hanging over [your] head like a halo" (Bazan). Fear is fundamentalist religion's most powerful tool.

And so, in using reason to try to undermine reason itself, fundamentalists sweep the scaffolding out from under their own feet, and yet claim to be standing in midair.

As an example, one of the central teachings in the Calvinist tradition I was raised in goes as follows: *The default state of every person from birth is "total depravity," a state of sinfulness deserving of eternal punishment in hell; God chooses (or "predestines") only certain people for salvation from this state, which occurs through belief in Jesus Christ as the savior; humans cannot believe and be saved apart from God's election (because they are "totally depraved"); and those who aren't saved are responsible and guilty for their own unbelief.* (See Romans 9, for instance, discussed later in this essay.) Armenian or "free-will" fundamentalists would disagree with this theology, but their version offers no better solution: *Everyone deserves hell, but everyone is "free" to choose God's salvation through belief in Jesus Christ.* Both doctrines are logically self-contradictory:

- In the first case, it is asserted that God is completely responsible for a person's salvation, and that each person is completely responsible for her own salvation. The two cannot simultaneously be true. The adamant fundamentalist, however, would refuse to admit this is a contradiction, and would only say it is a *seeming* contradiction; though our reason is not able to comprehend the infallible *Truth* given us in the Bible, we must accept it as the truth. (I personally know hundreds of people who hold this view; I grew up among them, I went to church and school with them, and this was a frequent topic in preaching, teaching, and discussion.)

- In the second case, it is asserted that humans are free to choose salvation, when in fact humans are *constrained* by situational and dispositional variables—not to mention by the rational contradictions of fundamentalist theology. Tough luck if you're born in the wrong part of the world and happen to be raised in the wrong religion or without religion, or if Christian theology doesn't elicit your belief; in either case you're destined for hell.

In addition to the internal logical contradictions of these doctrines, each also contradicts Christian teachings about God's goodness. Each doctrine presents a God who is ruthless in punishing souls eternally in hell, first creating them and then either only choosing certain people to be saved, or only accepting those fortunate enough to believe what God wants them to believe (without any real intervention on God's part, leaving it to evangelists and missionaries, who may or may not show up where you live, or may or may not convince you to believe). To assert God's goodness in either case is absurd, as God's character and actions (or *inactions*) contradict everything we comprehend in the term "good" (beneficence, desire for the best outcome for others, love, compassion, etc.).

The theological argument that "goodness" cannot be separated from the nature of God and applied as an exterior criterion to God's nature and actions is yet another example of a circular argument:

- It is asserted that if goodness is considered an exterior criterion, then it is made superior to God, and nothing can be superior to God. But this is rhetorical nonsense. Goodness is a description of a type of action or state of being; it is an abstract concept that allows us to characterize actions or beings. An abstract idea cannot rightly be said to exist in the same way a being exists, and therefore to assert that "goodness" would be superior to God if it were an external criterion is a faulty argument. Imagine arguing that *deciduousness* were "superior" to a tree because it is an outside criterion used to classify a type of tree. The idea of relative greatness or magnitude is not applicable, because one is not comparing two *beings*, but describing a being's characteristics by use of an abstract category.

- Furthermore, if *good = whatever God happens to be*, then to say that "God is good" is identical to saying "God is God," which contains no meaning other than "God is what God is." To call God "good," meaning "whatever God happens to be," and to claim God is worthy of praise and love because of that is absurd. If a "good" God creates human souls fallible, allows them to "fall," and punishes them eternally for it, then the word "good" has lost all meaning. (It also makes little sense for such a God to enter the world, suffer, and die, in the person of Jesus Christ, out of love for humankind. These two—equally biblical—portraits of God are mutually exclusive.)

I referred parenthetically to Romans 9 above. In context of a discussion of fundamentalist notions of God's goodness, it is a fitting time to consider the passage (focusing on verses 13–22):

> Just as it is written: "Jacob I loved, but Esau I hated."
>
> What then shall we say? Is God unjust? Not at all! For he says to Moses,
>
> "I will have mercy on whom I have mercy,
> and I will have compassion on whom I have compassion."
>
> It does not, therefore, depend on human desire or effort, but on God's mercy. For Scripture says to Pharaoh: "I raised you up for this very purpose, that I might display my power in you and that my name might be proclaimed in all the earth." Therefore God has mercy on whom he wants to have mercy, and he hardens whom he wants to harden.
>
> One of you will say to me: "Then why does God still blame us? For who is able to resist his will?" But who are you, a human being, to talk back to God? "Shall what is formed say to the one who formed it, 'Why did you make me like this?'" Does not the potter have the right to make out of the same lump of clay some pottery for special purposes and some for common use?
>
> What if God, although choosing to show his wrath and make his power known, bore with great patience the objects of his wrath—prepared for destruction?

Paul has made a poor metaphor here. In the biblical paradigm, Adam (cf. Hebrew *adamah*: "earth") was indeed formed from dust—but God breathed into that dust and conferred sentience, a mind, and a soul. A human is not insentient clay, but a being that feels and suffers. If the argument for God's morality is based on the comparison of a human to clay, therefore, it fails. A potter certainly has a right to make and destroy pottery; but does that potter have the right to beat a dog, or abuse a woman—or more to the point, give birth to a child with the intention of torturing it? Absolutely not.

Furthermore, it is absurd to assert that God must exercise "patience" with "objects" that God personally and intentionally "prepared for destruction." That would be like saying a potter intentionally made a cup with holes in it, and then nobly exhibited patience toward the offending vessel every time he tried to drink from the cup and found that it leaked.

Utter nonsense.

Paul's use of the word "mercy" in this passage likely requires explanation for those unfamiliar with the doctrine of original sin. The reason Paul believes it is merciful of God to select only some for favor is that the Bible asserts that each person is born automatically guilty and deserving of damnation because of The Fall (Adam and Eve's sin of eating the forbidden fruit in Eden, and the subsequent curse laid on them and their offspring by God). It won't take the reader long to grasp the absurdity of this doctrine, and I find it unworthy of detailed analysis here. Suffice it to say, as Bazan puts it, "in what medieval kingdom does justice work this way?"

Finally, in this passage Paul takes a cue from the Old Testament book of Job, and also cites Isaiah, when he writes:

> One of you will say to me: "Then why does God still blame us? For who is able to resist his will?" But who are you, a human being, to talk back to God? "Shall what is formed say to the one who formed it, 'Why did you make me like this?'"

As in the book of Job, the human attempt to reason with God regarding the most important questions is short-circuited by a simple power claim: "Who are you to ask questions of God?" In other words, God is so great and you are so small that you don't have the right to a response to your perfectly reasonable question of why humans are responsible for their sinfulness, when God made them that way in the first place ("Then why does God still blame us?"). David Bazan responds cuttingly to this situation:

from In Stitches

a shadow on the water
a whisper on the wind
on long walks with my daughter
who is lately full of questions
about you
when job asked you the question
you responded "who are you
to challenge your creator?"
well if that one part is true
it makes you sound defensive

like you had not thought it through
enough to have an answer
like you might have bit off
more than you could chew

The truth is that the Bible and fundamentalist theology do not have any answers for how the actions ascribed to God (making humans fallible and then blaming them for falling) could possibly be conceived as *just* or *good*. The only response is that one does not have the right to ask that question.

It was that very question, and the lack of any answer for it, that eventually, after years and years of inner turmoil, caused me to leave the fundamentalist Christian faith I grew up in. As Bazan puts it, "well if that one part is true / it makes you sound defensive / like you had not thought it through / enough to have an answer." I found no answers to my deepest questions in fundamentalist Christianity, finding only the rebuttals that human reason cannot be trusted, and that I didn't have the right to ask God such questions in the first place.

I have come to realize that two aspects of my mind had been at war from early childhood on: the cultural/psychological side and the rational side. The rational part of my mind was *never*, even as a young child, willing to accept the biblical doctrines of original sin and eternal punishment. But psychological fear of that same punishment—the fear that the most irrational and unjust thing I had ever heard or could imagine might actually be true, because everyone around me believed it so firmly—kept me constantly trying to convince myself to maintain the core beliefs I had been taught.

When I step back and consider the beliefs of fundamentalist Christians as if I hadn't been raised to believe them, I realize that they do not elicit my belief. They are self-contradictory and unreasonable, and are based on one primary faulty assumption—the infallibility of the Bible. If one leaves that premise behind, one is left with a religious tradition that, like all religious traditions, is full of moments of transcendent insight and inspiration, but also full of human flaws.

I am grateful to have evolved out of fundamentalism, to be able to see beauty and wisdom in all religions, retaining the ideas that are most reasonable and lovely, and discarding the dross.

The Purpose of Religious and Aesthetic Experience

As a teenager and young adult, I could never quite understand why so many of my friends at church expressed the desire for sermons that were "relevant" and "practical." That was rather the contrary of what I longed for in religion, and it struck me—for some as yet unarticulated reason—as antithetical to the authentic religious experience.

What I wanted in a religious service was lofty ideas, moving stories, poetic language. I wanted profundity, not practicality—not because I didn't want to live according to the Christian faith, but because I did want to live according to the Christian faith. I instinctively sensed that only inasmuch as my moral and aesthetic sensibilities were kindled and shaped by the literary rhetoric of scripture and the Christian tradition could I come to sense the rightness of the Christian way of life. I don't think I needed help deriving the religious and moral practicalities of everyday life from those higher principles of thought and feeling—rather, I needed those ideas and feelings to stir my soul and elevate my desires.

Religion, like art, most fully serves its purpose when it ennobles us through aesthetic experience. I don't look to religion to give me information about the specifics of what is right and wrong any more than I look to art and literature to do so. What I look to religion, art, and literature to do is to provide the experience of rightness, goodness, holiness itself. Only out of the moral and aesthetic sensibilities elicited this way can meaningful practical actions be chosen, practiced, and sustained.

It's easy enough to tell someone how to lose weight and live a healthy lifestyle—and entirely obvious to the majority of people, most likely even to the overweight person. It's not information that is lacking, and information often has little power to elicit the sustained desire and will to accomplish a way of life. What is lacking is a broader vision, a narrative and language in which the way of living becomes admirable and appears noble and right, thereby not only producing results but confering a sense of purpose and fulfillment throughout the arduous process toward those results.

The purpose of religion, like art, is to ennoble the heart and mind, and in so doing to bring proper and beneficent actions into being—consequently fulfilling not only the moral obligations of religious practice, but also fulfilling the individual's fundamental need for purpose that will sustain that practice.

Magnanimous Despair

For me, Advent means that God is coming into your life—is already there, in fact, has always been there, but you are about to experience that fact in an unprecedented way.

I used to think I had a pretty firm grasp of what that meant, having spent my first 25 years as a devoted member of a conservative, Protestant Christian tradition. Those years were never easy, and I had always been plagued with doubts and fears from early childhood on, but I never anticipated the traumatic loss of faith that I experienced in my 25th year. I won't go into great detail, but at age 25 my doubts became unrelenting. And suddenly the only framework I had ever had for understanding life and for making meaning was whisked away. This coincided with an event that sparked a resurgence of a longstanding anxiety disorder. The result was a year-long cycle of severe anxiety and depression unlike anything I had ever experienced. I was going through each day in terror and despair, literally shaking.

On one hand, I no longer believed in hell; on the other, I very much believed that I was destined for it because of my loss of faith and that I was experiencing only a foretaste of untold suffering in my anxiety and depression. This spiritual agony was exacerbated by an anxiety disorder I have had since I was very young as well as concomitant depression, which I had never before experienced.

My intention is not to elicit pity or to exaggerate my experience for dramatic effect. I simply want to give a context for the poem reprinted below—and, as unlikely as it may seem, to link it to the idea of advent.

Advent, as I said above, for me means God entering your life in an unprecedented way. I have come to view the experience of losing my faith and falling into anxiety and depression, into fear of damnation, into hopelessness, as being God's advent into my life. In that time, I often remembered some of those who had experienced the same kind of darkness I was undergoing. There was the ultimate example of Christ on the cross, when the Father turned His back, and I really should invoke that example more than any here, as I'm discussing the Christian idea of advent—but as you can imagine, that example was problematic for me in my loss of faith, and it often served only to increase my distress. Instead, I turned more often to the book of Job (please understand that I am not comparing myself to Christ or to Job, but my situation felt like a lesser parallel to those abandonments), the most distressed psalms, and to poets like George Herbert and Gerard Manley Hopkins. In "The Search," Herbert addresses God, writing, "Be not Almightie, let me say, / Against, but for me."[1] Hopkins writes, "O the mind, mind has mountains; cliffs of fall / Frightful, sheer, no-man-fathomed. Hold them cheap / May who ne'er hung there"[2] and "That night, that year / Of now done darkness I wretch lay wrestling with (my God!) my God".[3] There were others who had fallen into darkness, who had wrestled with God before me. This fact did not often feel like any consolation at all, but it did keep me from the danger of ultimate self-absorption—perhaps the primary danger for anyone undergoing anxiety or depression or trauma of any kind—thinking my situation utterly unique.

My situation was not unique, of course, and my sense of that was mediated through the work of poets, both ancient and more recent. And when I found myself able to write during this period of darkness, it was the styles of those poets that were meaningful to me that showed up in my own writing and enabled me to explore my own experience. For that reason, the styles of the sections of "Weak Devotions" are various; they are different ways of examining, thinking about, expressing my struggle; they are hands reaching out to those who have undergone similar struggles. Much of the poem was written over the course of the most acute period of my difficulty.

I have not returned to and do not anticipate returning to the kind of orthodox[4] Christian faith I once had. I do, however, in my better moments, believe in God and God's goodness, and say with Herbert, "if I imp my wing on thine, / Affliction shall advance the flight in me."[5] I have a very strong sense that I have been taken through these experiences. That sense has often caused me terror and anger, but I know that the way I think

1. Herbert, 154.

2. Hopkins, "[No worst, there is none . . .]," 100.

3. Ibid., "Carrion Comfort," 99.

4. i.e., "traditional," not "Orthodox"

5. Herbert, "Easter Wings," 38.

and feel has been changed and will never be the same, and out of my despair I have been brought to a place of faith, weak though it may be. Now perhaps I have some idea of what Andrew Marvell meant when he wrote, "Magnanimous Despair alone / Could show me so divine a thing, / Where feeble hope could ne'er have flown, / but vainly flapped its tinsel wing."[6]

We have faith; we lose faith. We have times of peace; we have times of great distress. And I have found that God enters life not only through belief but also through unbelief, not only through rejoicing but also through fear and outrage. As the angel says to Caedmon in Bede's *Historia Ecclesiastica*, "Nevertheless, you must sing."

Weak Devotions

I.

Why do You leave
some recess of my mind,
my heart, unlorded?
Leave nothing behind
that will linger in shit
and wallow and grind
itself in filthy defiance,
in masochistic, blind
groping after further
blasphemies. Furnace, kind
Lord, the furthest reaches
of me—make me refined.
Make me new. Take me to You.
Why have You assigned
this torture to me,
this desperate mind
that thinks inevitably
what it fears to think? Be kind
and do not let me be.
Need I remind
You, Lord, that You lay claim
to even the blindness of the purblind
worm—not only its righteous
wriggling? Be kind and be, kind
Lord, what You rightly are.
Rule what—whatsoever—you find.

6. Marvell, "The Definition of Love," 35.

Rein me in and reign in me.
There is freedom only when You bind.
Take me wholly, holy God.
Wholly, Holy. Mind my mind.

II.

As the deer pants for streams of water,
so my soul longs for You, O God.

I would rather be afflicted at Your hand forever
than be coddled by the hand of the devil.

I would rather be a doorkeeper in the house of my God
than dwell in the tents of the wicked.

I trust Your affliction, and hardship from Your hand gives me
    hope.
But the ease and luxuries of the evil one I despise.

My soul thirsts for God, for the living God.

All Your waves and breakers have swept over me.

III.

Religion is a Crutch

but not at first—first it is the diagnosis
and the medication prescribed,
it is the scalpel and the surgeon's hand,
it is the surgery and the hospital bed,
the death of anesthesia and the waking up.
And yes it is the crutch by which one heals
and learns to walk and live all over again.
And you say *crutch* as if it were an easy thing.

IV.

In my mind there is a population of squirrels
in a field of doubt, each one a question
about You. They are not pretty squirrels.
They are mangy, trembling things with teeth.
They are rummaging in the grass and darting

up and down the trees, gnawing and twitching.
But when they feel the wind of Your passing,
they freeze where they are and lean back on their haunches,
hands folded in front, asking forgiveness.
They become so beautiful I forget they're mine.

V.

Sometimes I'm afraid that I am damned
by God. Such blasphemies have entered my mind
as I dare not repeat for fear of making others stumble.
And once something enters my mind,
I have to wonder if it originated in my heart.
(Let it not be so!)
                        Sometimes the only relief
is this feeling that, even if I were damned,
I would say: If it be Your will, may it be so.
Is this something someone who was damned
would say—or hope to say?

VI.

Our holiest act is to enter into mystery,
just as God's holiest act was to enter
into mortal flesh, into death—
the only mystery available to Him.

VII.

The Harrowing

not of Hell only, but of the earth,
and not in strength of arms, but in assumed
vulnerability, in mortal flesh,
in sacrifice. What kind of God creates
a world that will necessitate His own
suffering, His harrowing of Himself?
That God and no other would I have
harrow my heart and be hallowed in it.

VIII.

Sometimes I don't want to praise You, Lord.
I'd rather let the stones cry out
and see if they can shame me into song,

rid me of my muting doubt.
Here's my voice in praise—though it seems wrong
for You to prefer my stony song to the stones' accord.

IX.

Spring again.
                    Rain showers beat the dogwood and lilac.
            Glory petals strew the path
                                of my undeserving.

He does not treat us as our sins deserve
            or repay us according to our iniquities.

~

The next day, I walk by again.
            The petals are sliming in the sun,
stricken with flies,
                                and the world is briefly
            telling the truth about me.

X.

and if in spring it suddenly turns

                cold and a dead brown leaf scritches

        against a branch
                                what
        harsh thing
                        are You saying to me

                over and again

XI.

My heart is creaturely before You.

And if I am full of anger, have mercy.
And if I am crooked, remember me.
And if my thoughts are (all my thinking isisis)
perverse, release me.
And if I know love only from a fearful distance,

take me to You, writhing and undone.

I do not want I want I want I want
(kicking and yelping) Your law,
a leash around my neck. (Have mercy.)
Without it I am not fit for company.
Do not leave me
feral and alone—yank
my heart that it may come heeling
and creaturely before You.

XII.

Remember my partitioned
hearts, sevenly seeking to
love You, little seats for Your
smallest mercies to topple
in their lightest sitting down.

XIII.

I grew older. The terrors of my childhood—
anxious days, sleepless nights weeping,
gasping for breath, afraid of the strangeness
of death and afraid of the strangeness
of existence—became mostly a memory.
I thought I had become a man.
I thought I had learned how to live.
But You said, Look, you are a child again,
and in that moment I suffered Your terrors anew,
and they did not end. Week one. Week two. Week three.
Over and over I despaired of peace, of life itself.
You said, Look, you are a child again.
And in my self-pity and in my anger
I was not listening. You terrified me,
You terrified me, You brought me down
into the pit. And You said, Look,
you are a child again. And I said,
How dare You? I cannot endure.
And You said, Nevertheless.
And I said, Why? And I raged
and I shook and I wept for weeks,
and then I fell silent in my despair.
And You said, Look, you are a child again,

and now you can call me Father.

XIV.

I have envied, yes,
the dog that cannot think of hell—
I have envied the dust mite,
the palm tree and the stone.
And can I say
(can I tell You something
I've never told You before?)
that I have envied nonthings
because they do not exist.

XV.

There is so much anger in me
because we are mortal and suffer
in body and soul—
I am full of bile,

but won't You turn it into sweetness?
If You can make honey
in the carcass of a lion,
can't You do this in me?

XVI.

Though there is a sorrow comes
that cannot be dissuaded,
and a fear that will not subside,
beauty insists—
                little imperfect trumpet
of God's glory blown into purple bloom
on the chain-link fence. And you see it.

Exorcism

When I was young, about 8 or 9, my pastor performed an exorcism on me. It was late one night after my parents called him in what must have been desperation during another of my innumerable episodes of terror. I woke them almost nightly for years, ashamedly but desperately creeping into their room to shake an arm or touch a leg, hoping my dad would come and sit with me as I cried, as he often did, while I struggled for breath, panicked and sickened yet again at the thought of death and—more than that—of hell. I was tormented, and I don't say that lightly.

After calling our pastor to ask him to meet and pray with me, my parents drove me to the church, where we met him and his wife in the empty sanctuary (as some Christians call the room where services are held). It seemed huge to me at that age, especially when it was empty, and especially that night, enveloped in darkness, possessed suddenly of a hushed and nocturnal aspect previously unknown to me.

The four adults "laid hands on"[1] me and prayed. Then Pastor Bob— we did call him "Pastor Bob," and I don't remember anyone ever referring to him by his last name—decided to have me stand up and asked the others to step aside. He stood in front of me with a little glass jar of oil. He asked me to stand with my mouth open. I remember being confused and scared, not to mention embarrassed, and I felt I might cry at any moment. This made keeping my mouth open difficult, and I felt vulnerable and foolish standing there, mouth hanging open. But I did trust this man, a major symbol of authority—of God's authority—for me, and I trusted my parents. So I tried to follow his instructions carefully.

Pastor Bob began to wet his fingers with the oil and to sprinkle oil over my body from a distance of five feet or so, and he began to call out in

1. A phrase of biblical origin (Hebrews 6:2) frequently used in evangelical Christianity. It indicates a prayer ritual in which the intercessors place their hands on the person being prayed for, usually reserved for crises or other significant occasions.

a loud and commanding voice, speaking to the supposed demon in order to ascertain whether there was actually one there. I remember his words, at least roughly: "I command you, evil spirit, in the name and in the authority of Jesus Christ to speak your name. *What is your name?*" He had instructed me to just keep my mouth open, but not to speak purposely, so I stood there, waiting fearfully for a phantom voice to rise from my own throat.

He was insistent and persisted at this for several minutes. Finally, he told me to speak the first word that came to my mind. There was nothing there. I felt like something was going wrong. I didn't know what to do, but I felt that I had to say something. I made up a word, a sound that was not a word. The adults left the room briefly to discuss this utterance and determine whether it was meaningful or revelatory. They returned, having concluded that it was not the name of a demon, and that I could rest in the certainty that I was a child of God and that I no longer needed live in fear. Pastor Bob's wife gave me a toy police badge that I was to keep in order to remind myself that I was a child of the King, a deputy in God's kingdom, and that I could take out that badge whenever a "spirit of fear" came over me. I remember crying a lot, and I don't know what particular emotion caused it, I was experiencing so many—relief, fear, exhaustion, disorientation, doubt, embarrassment, hope—all simultaneous in me.

My parents drove me home. We passed silently through the quiet town, its sections of antique red brick roads lined with great oaks and magnolias, past the zoo with its sleeping lions whose roars I had heard daily when we lived in town, across the bridge over the ever-muddy Red River, past Lake Buhlow where they raced high-speed motor boats, past the creosote plant and VA hospital into the hilly outlying town of Pineville, over the railroad tracks, past the cattle farm on Road Gully Road, into our neighborhood and upstairs to my bed, where I swooned at last into sleep.

The Way They Loved Each Other

On July 14, 2011 I was verbally and physically assaulted in a parking lot at a local grocery store by four people because they thought that my shorts were too short and that I looked like a "faggot." They didn't try to take any money. They didn't try to steal the beer I had just bought. They only wanted to hurt someone. And so they left me with a swollen face and jaw and a black eye, with a confused mind and troubled heart. I was up all night with pain, nausea, and roiling emotions. I eventually decided I should go to the ER. Three fractures in my face.

Below is a poem I wrote about the incident. I don't feel anger against the perpetrators, only confusion and pity and sadness. I also don't take credit for not feeling anger. It's simply the natural course my mind and heart have taken. But I will say that it has allowed me to recover psychologically from the incident in a way that I don't believe would have been possible if I were plagued by anger and desire for vengeance. I'm grateful for this grace.

The Way They Loved Each Other

What to be more astonished at:
my calm as the fist made contact
and I saw a flash of white
and the world went silent
as if I had stepped out of it
momentarily, only to be brought back
with a rush of sound and visible objects—
the way I asked them to help me
find my glasses, expecting them
(even as they taunted me,
even though they had just assaulted me)
to feel underneath the violent tribal urge
the obligations of empathy—
the way even as one of them found my glasses

and smashed them again on the ground
I refused to believe that was really
what he wanted to do—the way
they loved each other
in the most primitive manner
but loved each other nonetheless
despite feeling the need to punish a "faggot"
who did not dress like them, because
he did not dress like them—
the way tears and nausea overwhelmed me
nightlong much more than had the blow itself—
the way such small suffering can feel
unbearable—the way no strength is found
for what seems to have no explanation,
a troubled mind more harmful
to the body than fractured bones.

III. Interviews

An Interview at
American Literary Review

Justin Bigos: Your first book of poems, *Weak Devotions*, contains a fifteen–part sequence of the same title. The sequence as well as the book contain much conversation with God, often interrogating His motives—even His very authority. What is the human cost of entering this mysterious place of devotion—as God once entered the mystery of "mortal flesh," "his holiest act"? Is a "weak devotion" the closest we humans come to something holy?

Luke Hankins: Yehuda Amichai writes in his poem "Relativity":

> Someone told me he's going down to Sinai because
> he wants to be alone with his God:
> I warned him.[1]

Indeed.

You ask what the human cost of entering "the mysterious place of devotion" is. In my experience, it is very high. And judging by what poets devoted to God throughout the ages have written, I think they would agree. But I don't think anyone enters a devout life counting the cost—not even monastics and ascetics (which I certainly have never been). That's because one can't imagine or begin to comprehend the actual price until it's already being exacted. Hopkins, in "Carrion Comfort," writes:

> But ah, but O thou terrible, why wouldst thou rude on me
> Thy wring-world right foot rock? lay a lionlimb against me?[2]

The psalmist(s) of Psalm 42 write(s):

> Deep calls to deep
> in the roar of your waterfalls;

1. Amichai, 141.
2. Hopkins, 99.

all your waves and breakers
have swept over me.[3]

Some, from a perspective outside of religious or spiritual devotion, would undoubtedly say that the cost is high because the devout are fooling themselves, chasing after shadows and myths and confronting their own neuroses in the dark, working themselves into a frenzy seeking what was never there to begin with. This is certainly not a novel idea for anyone who has ever genuinely sought the divine. (E.g., see R. S. Thomas' poem "Threshold.") Whom do you meet in the desert? Is it the Maker in whom you see all of your fears and all of your hopes embodied, or is it the Nothing in which you see only a reflection of your own inexplicable being? And which is more terrifying?

But though the cost of entering this desert is undoubtedly high, you come away changed irrevocably—which may be worth having experienced that "dark night of the soul." As Andrew Marvell writes:

Magnanimous Despair alone
Could show me so divine a thing,
Where feeble Hope could ne'er have flown
But vainly flapped its tinsel wing.[4]

I grew up in an evangelical, conservative Christian environment, and I clung desperately to that faith for most of my life, through constant cycles of doubt and belief. *Weak Devotions*, and particularly the title poem, chronicles the doubt and belief that has always been interwoven in my life, and more recently the evolution away from traditional religious beliefs toward—what?—a deeper acknowledgment of mystery and uncertainty. This, for me, was a very traumatic transition, in which I felt that my framework for understanding life was torn away, leaving me floating in a void. This spiritual transition coincided with a year–long period of intense and unremitting anxiety, a psychological problem I've dealt with since early childhood that suddenly burst out of control, and a mercifully shorter period of depression—a depth I hope to never touch again with so much as my little toe.

I realize that to write poems about this subject risks alienating any readers who have no experience with a religious upbringing or, on the other hand, with primal and deep–seated religious beliefs of their own. My hope

3. Psalm 42:7.
4. Marvell, 35.

in this respect is that something like what T. S. Eliot has said about George Herbert's poetry might prove true of poetry like mine as well (not to in any way compare the quality of my poems with that of Herbert's!):

> When I claim a place for Herbert among those poets whose work every lover of English poetry should read and every student of English poetry should study, irrespective of religious belief or un-belief, I am not thinking primarily of the exquisite craftsmanship, the extraordinary metrical virtuosity, or the verbal felicities, but of the *content* of the poems which make up *The Temple*. These poems form a record of spiritual struggle which should touch the feeling, and enlarge the understanding of those readers also who hold no religious belief and find themselves unmoved by religious emo-tion. (italics Eliot's)[5]

Finally, you ask whether a "weak devotion" is the closest we as humans may come to something holy. My response is that we as humans do not come to what is holy at all. In my (of course subjective) experience, I see the opposite as true: the holy comes to us, and we can never be ready for it. (The holy is always other—etymologically, the word implies that which is whole, complete, inviolate—unlike us.) Our weak devotion is a reaction more than it is an action. In the poem of mine you quote, I do write of entering into mystery, but that is in itself a response to a prompting from outside. Those who enter the desert do not do it of their own volition, but are driven there by the wind of the Spirit. If it were up to us, I think none of us would ever go. We don't want the terror, the pain, the annihilation of the self. But it seems that the Holy sees fit to drive some to that point—not all, and perhaps not even many. Why this is, I couldn't say. I happen to believe that the will behind this is beneficent, only because of having come through my small version of the experience. Had you asked me during the most try-ing periods, you would have been met with silence, or worse. But now, like Marvell, I do in my better moments believe despair to be magnanimous.

JB: For such a serious book, I love when your strange humor arrives, such as in the poem "Portrait of Myself as a Barbarian." The poem exists in "some barbarous century / long before the invention / of eyeglasses," and the speaker makes his way through the world, laughing, even as the unseen wolves advance. I thought I was the only one with the private fantasy/fear of living in a time without corrective lenses, since my vision is horrible. The

---

5. Eliot, 239.

poem pleases me with its vulnerability and fortitude, and I wonder if it's between those two things that humor sometimes appears. So: can we bring humor to the table when having our sit–downs with God?

LH: You mention humor in "our sit–downs with God," and I immediately think of the character Tevye in the musical "Fiddler on the Roof." What a marvelous example of humor in conversation with the divine! Well, Tevye's kind of humor requires a nonchalance and self–confidence that I don't naturally possess. But there are so many kinds of humor, and perhaps the one I most appreciate in poetry arises from the kind of irony we see in Emily Dickinson, W. H. Auden, Elizabeth Bishop, or, more recently, Kay Ryan, in which a grave subject is spoken of in a relatively lighthearted way, which can paradoxically increase the emotional impact of the poem once the serious underpinnings of the humor are recognized. I hope to include more poems with this kind of humor in my next book. Here's one small example of the kind of humor I'm talking about in one of my newer poems, in its entirety:

On Judgment

In canine mythology,
Sisyphus is the most blessèd of all,
granted an eternal game of fetch.

The humor of a dog's perspective on mythology, and on the myth of Sisyphus in particular, is obvious. But I hope that the poem also works on a deeper level, in which it comments on the way one's perspective and state of mind can make hell of heaven and heaven of hell—the way that what we now view as a curse we might one day learn to see as a blessing.

JB: One of my favorite poems in the book is the villanelle "A Shape with Forty Wings," which will appear in the next issue of *American Literary Review*. I'm curious how long it took you to write this poem. I have tried many villanelles over the years, and I have never written a good one. Do you need to have strong repeating lines right away, or can those come later? (Your terrific repeating lines are: "Love is strange and calls me to stranger things" and "I've drawn my life—a shape with forty wings.")

LH: As with most of my poems, I wrote the initial poem fairly quickly, then over a period of several years came back to it and revised it numerous times.

In this case, the refrains came first. I think that it's helpful to have a meter in mind if you decide to come up with refrain lines first, so that instead of pulling words out of thin air you at least have some sort of framework—a length of utterance, at least—to drop them into. Here, it's pentameter, but there are no restrictions on which meter is required in a villanelle, though pentameter has historically been a favorite in English–language villanelles.

But there is no right or wrong way to compose a poem, whether free verse or "formal." We all work on finding what works for us—and of course what worked for us once or a dozen times may not work for the next poem, and we may have to try new strategies. The important thing is to be willing to be flexible, and once you have something on the page, to be able to achieve a level of objectivity in assessing its success or lack thereof.

JB: I know you have spoken and written about this before, including on American Public Media's program "On Being," but I wonder if you'd be willing to discuss yet one more time the assault you suffered last summer. For readers who don't know: you were assaulted by four people in July of 2011; the perpetrators called you "faggot" and made fun of the way you were dressed, and they did not attempt to steal your money or car. This was clearly a hate crime. The attack took place in Asheville, North Carolina, a city that prides itself on its liberal—and especially pro–gay—values. You've written a poem, "The Way They Loved Each Other,"[6] about the event, and one of the things I admire about it is that the speaker recognizes a love in the attackers, even if "tribal," "primal." But I also admire that you were able to write such a gracious poem so quickly after the event. People sometimes make fun of poetry that seems written as therapy, but what else can a poem like yours do but attempt to heal—both yourself and the world? Are people unfair when they mock the poem of therapy, or is there a difference between therapy and art?

LH: The difficulty with comparing art and therapy is on one level merely a semantic one: we have certain associations with the sterile and history–laden word "therapy" that we are—rightly, I suppose—loath to bring into a conversation about art. Art—indeed, beauty itself—is perennially therapeutic. We might prefer the terms restorative, or calming, or invigorating, or pleasure–inducing, or any number of terms that indicate the very real physiological and psychological effects of the aesthetic experience of objects, sounds, and ideas. But regardless of how we describe it, it's true that

6. See pp. 145–146 of this volume.

we often change for the better through our aesthetic experiences. I know beyond a shadow of a doubt that this has been true for me—so much so that the word "therapy" is quite reductive.

Writing the poem about the assault I experienced was primarily an attempt on my part to understand those who had attacked me, and by doing so to understand what seemed to me an inexplicable event. You're right that the assailants didn't try to steal anything. They apparently had no motive other than to hurt someone they perceived as different from themselves. And that was the most difficult aspect of the event to deal with. It filled me with inexpressible sorrow and anxiety, not only for myself but also for them. The pain of the fractured bones in my face was intense, but my inability to comprehend why or how these people could have acted this way was by far the more traumatizing aspect. I was sad not only for my experience, but for the lives of the people who had chosen to do this to me. What must their lives be like for this to be how they spent their time? But by making something out of the confusion and pain, I felt that I was able to re-deem the experience and instead of dwelling on how it had hurt me or how inexplicable others' actions were, I attempted to come to an understanding of their actions as human, as not other but as familiar. Joseph Conrad has said something marvelous in his famous "Preface":

> [The artist] speaks to our capacity for delight and wonder, to the sense of mystery surrounding our lives; to our sense of pity, and beauty, and pain; to the latent feeling of fellowship with all creation—and to the subtle but invincible conviction of solidar-ity that knits together the loneliness of innumerable hearts: to the solidarity in dreams, in joy, in sorrow, in aspirations, in illusions, in hope, in fear, which binds men [sic] to each other, which binds together all humanity—the dead to the living and the living to the unborn.[7]

Making art is essential to who we are as humans—we are artificers, makers, shapers. And through shaping words or paint or musical notes many of us sense that we are fully engaging with what it means to be human—and we are able to come to a fuller understanding of what it means for others to be human as well—a conviction of what Conrad calls our "solidarity."

In the Christian tradition, humans are made "in the image of God," and since God is the great Maker, we as reflections of the divine are also makers. For me this is one of the most beautiful and most essential Christian

7. Conrad, 120.

teachings. We make because we are made. We are made because God loves to make. We are the result of the pleasureful work of the divine. And we sense this most, perhaps, when we are ourselves engaged in the pleasureful work of making art.

An Interview at *Connotation Press:*
An Online Artifact

Monica Mankin: When and why did you decide to translate poetry? Can you talk a little about your process for translating poetry? I mean, I've encountered various attitudes toward poetry translation over the years. Some people believe it can't really be done, that the poem can only truly exist in its original language and in the forms of that language. Other people, and clearly you are part of this camp, believe that the poem can translate. What is it that has to translate? To elaborate on this question: Radulescu "asserts that 'there is always something mysterious about the [French] language.'" What do you understand her to mean by this statement? Do you agree with her assertion? As you work to translate her poetry from the eternally mysterious French language into the English language, how do you translate the mystery? How do you preserve the essence of meaning that the original language creates within a poem?

Luke Hankins: The poet Basil Bunting famously said that "poetry is a sound." I never agree with hyperbolic, reductive statements like this—however, they can be useful for emphasis. It is true that the greatest poets are highly attentive to sound, and the best readers of poetry are as well. The more one reads and writes, the more one can become aware of many effects that the very sound of language has on one's emotional and even intellectual responses, effects that go largely unnoticed unless one trains oneself to attend to them.

Stella is clearly, in my opinion, intensely attuned to the nuances of language, both its sound and its sense (and its *silence* and its *nonsense*). There's a reason she writes poetry—in three languages, no less!—and there's a reason she studied philology (an older term for linguistics)—and this is probably the same reason that she finds it impossible, or at least undesirable, to translate her own poetry (though, thankfully, she does offer input on my translations). Consider, for instance, the violent extremes of tactile response to language in "a cry in the snow":

> I want to remain silent but my cry attaches itself
> to a sliver of light
>
> the snow covers it
> with its suffocating coolness   a loving gesture
> before the cold
>
> in the burning mouth

In many other poems (not included here in *Connotation Press*), words take on very physical manifestations. This happens all the time in both her French and her English poems (and, I assume, in her Romanian ones as well, though I can't read Romanian)—to such an extent and with such passionate insistence that I actually believe her when she writes in another poem I've translated, "I was afraid of vowels their paleness."

What does this mean for the endeavor of translation? The essential issue is that of *meaning*. Meaning is incredibly complex—far more complex than we could ever understand or articulate—and sound is a way of meaning, just as appearances are a way of meaning in visual art. This is especially true of poetry because of the degree of intentional use of sound, though it is vital in prose as well, sometimes as much so as in poetry. (Genre distinctions are counterproductive to this discussion, so I'll leave those behind.) I think, therefore, that we have to say that, in an ultimate sense, the meaning of a work in translation is not the same as the meaning of the original. The sound of the English translation is not the sound of the French original. There are, however, degrees of similarity in meaning (including elements of sound), and I happen to be rather old-fashioned in terms of the idea of being "faithful" to the original text—which means, for me, approximating my perception of the meaning of the original as closely as I can in English, and using whatever strategies best allow for that. But, in a sense, a translation is always a unique work in itself. It can be usefully viewed as a collaboration between text and translator (even when the original author is not involved) producing a novel work that is related as closely as possible to the original.

Is this endeavor worthwhile? Well, threaten lovers of literature with the removal of their native-language versions of *Don Quixote* or Wyslawa Szymborska's poems or Rilke's *Duino Elegies*, and see how they respond! The value, to me, is self evident. But the value is not simplistic and should not be misunderstood as inhering in a "reproduction" of the original text. A translation is a movement across and between languages, and if the old adage of something being "lost in translation" is true, it's equally true that many things are *gained* in translation. A translation means in a different way than the original, but that does not imply that it means *less* than the original. For these reasons, we are richer for having a large variety of translations of any given text available in our native languages.

I see that I've neglected the question about Stella's idea of there being something mysterious about the French language. I don't doubt that that is absolutely true for her. And I think that's all she means—for her, there is something mysterious about the language, and that's why it is "the language of poetry" for her. I don't think she's claiming that there's something inherently mysterious for all people about the French language as opposed to other languages. All language is mysterious, in fact, its workings subtle and invisible, its origins ancient and shadowed—in the view of many, it is literally a link between the material world and the spiritual. This is true of English just as much as it is true of French, just as much as it is true of every language. I'm only grateful that Stella writes poetry in the language that is for her most endowed with mystery and power. We're beneficiaries of her sensitivity to that language. It's something to be admired and to be sought after in the languages that we use ourselves. There is great power and great richness in developing that kind of sensitivity. Why do we think literature exists, after all? It is a reaching toward mystery, an embrace of mystery rather than an attempt to do away with it.

MM: The colon appears prominently in these poems. For instance, the poem "first mornings" concludes, ": the men who set out at sunrise to meet their lives." We see the colon again in "a cry in the snow (2)": ": there is still a cadaver to identify / : there is still a life to live and then from which direction will the snow / begin its white its long funeral." And also it sets off a list in "posthumous inventory": ": the evening like a buffalo / : the sea like a breath / : your face like a candle." How do you feel the colon working in these poems? Additionally, you have chosen to adhere to the formal appearance of the original poems. What sorts of challenges did that present for you? Can you speak to any favorable moments those challenges produced?

LH: Ah, don't think I haven't noticed the way you've incorporated colons into your question about colons! Well played! But seriously, in my view,

Stella uses the colon to increase silence. I think language has a multitude of silences that are essential parts of language itself. A certain kind of silence can be achieved with linebreaks in a poem. When one comes to a linebreak, there is a moment of silence, a break in the stream of words, a blank space. If a colon were placed at the end of a line, it would not have the effect of increasing the silence but would simply be incorporated into the silence already there. (Notice that this occurs once in "posthumous inventory.") But when you come to one of Stella's colons at the head of a line, it takes you by surprise—you're expecting the stream of words to continue. Instead, what you get is a meaningful silence added to a meaningful silence.

> I shout my sovereign cry
> which smashes the silence
>
> : there is still a cadaver to identify
> : there is still a life to live and then from which direction
>   will the snow
> begin its white its long funeral

As for the appearance of the poems on the page, yes, I have tried to approximate that appearance most of the time in English. In some poems not included here, I have taken more liberty with some of Stella's techniques, such as the way she adds whitespace between words on the same line. I have sometimes included whitespace in English where there is none in French because of differences in the way the English syntax operates. But my aim is always to achieve an effect that is as faithful to the effect of the original (its effect on *me*, I should say, in order to acknowledge subjectivity here) as possible. Oftentimes, I find that it's possible to remain very close to the shape of Stella's poems. This is due partly to the fact that her poems are largely fragmentary, containing many lists of nouns and many (so-called) incomplete sentences that don't require as much syntactical reordering as longer, more linear sentences would. The experience is very different from my experience translating the prose of Philippe Jaccottet, for instance, in which a lot of reordering and reshaping of sentences is necessary (see my translation, "Blazon in Green and White," in *New England Review* #31.3, for instance).

Still, translation always poses challenges, and approximating the shape of the original poems is only possible because of innumerable small changes in terms of which syntactical units appear where. I'll look at one tercet from "a cry in the snow" as a brief example. Here it is in Stella's French and in my English:

> ma présence semble causer l'inquiétude
> des roses
> dans le jardin

> ~

> my presence
> seems to make the roses tremble
> in the garden

As you can see from this example, it's not entirely accurate to say, as you put it, that I have "adhere[d] to the formal pattern of the poems." In order to remain what I call "faithful" in this instance, I felt that I had to both maintain the three-line stanza and attempt to use linebreaks in a way that would emphasize what is emphasized in the French. Thus, I want "l'inquiétude" at the end of a line at all costs, as it seems vital to me in terms of the effect of this stanza. On the other hand, ending a line on "les roses" seems less significant to me. (You can see how this is subjective and how another reader/translator might have a different perspective.) There is no way to (1) maintain the long initial line in the stanza, (2) maintain a linebreak on "l'inquiétude," *and* (3) retain the three-line stanza without wrenching the English out of order or having undesirable lines (e.g., "in the / garden"), creating effects that would be antithetical to the effect the French text would have on a native-language reader. So, I had to let the idea of a long initial line go. In translating, you have to prioritize; you have to let some elements go for the sake of more important ones. I chose the elements that were most significant for me, and the shape of the stanza was dictated by the means of expressing those elements. This is the case for every stanza, every line, every word of a translated poem.

MM: Which are your favorite lines from these Radulescu poems? Why?

LH: Some of my favorite lines are these from "posthumous inventory":

> consciousness awakening   the pillow sinks
> in a dreamlake

and these from "a cry in the snow (2)":

> : there is still a life to live and then from which direction will the
>   snow
> begin its white its long funeral

What draws me to the first set of lines is the contrary, simultaneous motion: consciousness awakening and the pillow sinking in a dreamlake at the same moment. To me, it conveys the sensation of waking, but waking into a dream. I also am fond of using *dreamlake* as a single word as a translation of "l'étang d'un rêve"—it seems just out of the ordinary enough, just weird enough to convey the strangeness of the moment in this poem. The second set of lines is striking to me primarily for the figure of snowfall as a funeral ritual, which I think is apt because of the quietness that we associate with snow. (Notice how the violence of the sound in the title "a cry in the snow" and in the first poem of that title is intensified because of this association.) Snow can muffle the landscape and accumulate quietly, falling more slowly than rain, so that it can indeed seem mournful.

I also think the ending of "a cry in the snow (2)" is especially powerful, though I couldn't articulate exactly what it means—perhaps *because* I can't articulate exactly what it means, yet I sense the effect of the line emotionally. This is one of many ways in which a poem can embody mystery—when a poem strikes us as *true* or *right* but eludes our attempts to adequately articulate why. I hope that it's clear that when I say "mystery"—both here and in my earlier response—the sense of the word for me is infused with its use in religious contexts, where it means not something that is hidden, but in fact something that is *revealed* but cannot be fully explained or exhaustively comprehended.

MM: Thank you very much for your time. I've really enjoyed reading these poems.

LH: This conversation has been a pleasure. Thank you for publishing these translations. Stella and I are both honored to appear here.

~

Translator's Note

Stella Vinitchi Radulescu was born in Romania, and left the country permanently in 1983, at the height of Ceausescu's communist regime. After seeking political asylum in Rome, she immigrated to the U.S. She received an M.A. in French from the University of Illinois at Chicago, and a Ph.D. in Philology from the University of Bucharest. She has taught French, first at Loyola University, then at Northwestern, since 1989.

Radulescu began writing poetry in Romanian at an early age and published several collections in Romania. As she puts it, "Writing poetry was risky—it could have been 'a political manifesto' against the regime!—but it was also a refuge." She faced a crisis of sorts when she left Romania because she was uncertain how to continue writing in a new language. However, she discovered that she could write in English and enjoyed discovering other dimensions of expression through writing in a new language. She attributes part of her success in this area to her study of philology. She also began to write in French, which was always "la langue de la poésie" for her. She points to the fact that Samuel Beckett wanted to write deliberately in French, and asserts that "there is always something mysterious about the language."

For Radulescu, it is difficult to translate her own poems. As she puts it, "I feel, think, act, perceive, smell, touch differently according to the language I write in." She has been kind enough to allow me to begin translating her French poetry, and I gratefully acknowledge her partnership in finalizing the translations which appear here.

These poems are selected and translated from *Un cri dans la neige* [*A cry in the snow*], winner of the Grand Prix de Poésie Noël-Henri Villard 2008, awarded by the Société des Poètes et Artistes de France. Radulescu received the Grand Prix "Art et Poésie" from the same organization in 2007 for her book, *Terre interrompue*, and is the recipient of the 2013 Prix Amélie Murat. Her numerous English volumes of poetry are represented in *I Scrape the Window of Nothingness: New & Selected Poems* (Orison Books, 2015).

Poems by Stella Vinitchi Radulescu

translated from the French by Luke Hankins

premiers matins

aussitôt l'aube
accouplement des saisons   la terre se réchauffe

le texte se lit à genoux

entre les pierres agenouillée la mer

premiers matins du monde matins lisses
matins de guerre

froid et chaleur   on va entrer dans nos maisons
de chair
les mains tendues comme de vastes horizons

on va goûter de ces lèvres
ce qui s'écrit   l'écume d'une vague la nonchalance
des signes—

comme je m'avance et mets le pied sur le jour
je vois des formes qui se dilatent
dans le miroir des heures

: les hommes qui partent au petit matin à la rencontre
de leurs vies

first mornings

at the break of dawn
juncture of the seasons   the earth warms

the text is read on one's knees

the sea kneeling between stones

the world's first mornings smooth mornings
mornings of war

cold and heat   we will enter our houses
of flesh
hands spread like vast horizons

we will taste what is written
on these lips   the foam of a wave the nonchalance
of gestures—

as I advance and step into daylight
I see forms expanding
in the mirror of the hours

: the men who set out at sunrise to meet
their lives

un cri dans la neige

au ras de la nuit
un feu éclate un bras me fait signe

ma présence semble causer l'inquiétude
des roses
dans le jardin

la révolte des oiseaux des tremblements
de terre

les rues s'allongent   l'ombre d'un mot
infini
hante les minutes hante

les heures
je veux me taire mais mon cri s'accroche
à un brin de lumière

la neige le couvre
de sa fraîcheur l'étouffe   un geste d'amour
d'avant le froid

dans la brûlure de la bouche

a cry in the snow

at the brim of night
a fire leaps up an arm gestures to me

my presence
seems to make the roses tremble
in the garden

and make the birds rise up
and make the earth shake

the streets lengthen   the shadow of an infinite
word
haunts the minutes haunts

the hours
I want to remain silent but my cry attaches itself
to a sliver of light

the snow covers it
with its suffocating coolness   a loving gesture
before the cold

in the burning mouth

un cri dans la neige (2)

je crie mon cri souverain
qui défonce le silence

: il reste un cadavre à nommer
: il reste une vie à vivre et puis de quel côté la neige
va commencer ses blanches ses longues funérailles

j'avance sans mémoire j'ai un nouveau corps
j'adore sa nudité   imaginez le vase ce temps
d'albâtre

qui sans lumière aucune vous déchire les yeux

a cry in the snow (2)

I shout my sovereign cry
which smashes the silence

: there is still a cadaver to identify
: there is still a life to live and then from which direction will the
     snow
begin its white its long funeral

I walk forward without memory I have a new body
I love its nakedness imagine the vase time
in alabaster

which without any light dazzles your eyes

inventaire posthume

1

un homme suspendu à une rose sa gorge
qui brûle
la clé oubliée sous la porte
                              la pluie
et l'après-midi

trois pétales et les mots pour les dire
l'habitude de chanter sa vie
ce qui s'arrondit ce qui va de soi fléchit
s'articule

l'incertitude d'être ici parmi tant de choses
qu'il faut nommer

: le soir comme un buffle
: la mer comme un souffle
: ton visage comme une bougie
une rue à droite l'autre au ciel hélas

applaudissez
l'amour qui se cache dans les gares
les couleurs pâles
les amants en fleur jonquilles cerisiers

les grands déserts

le clair-obscur

2

la conscience se réveille   l'oreiller sombre
dans l'étang d'un rêve

le quotidien met son chapeau de paille :

une belle journée passée en compagnie des hommes

3

la neige va fondre je vais me taire
vous allez piailler dans vos tombes les verbes
vont rouler libres sur la page quelqu'un
va parler comme un dieu quelque chose
va s'appeler ville
ou sable
nous allons chercher abri dans une conque

si légers si légers

presque impondérables . . .

posthumous inventory

1

a man suspended from a rose his throat
burns
the key forgotten under the door
                              the rain
and the afternoon

three petals and the words for them
the habit of singing one's life
that which polishes itself that which goes without saying
bends, articulates

the uncertainty of being here among so many things
that must be named

: the evening like a buffalo
: the sea like a breath
: your face like a candle
a street to the right the other in the sky alas

applaud
love which hides itself in the train stations
the pale colors
the lovers in bloom   daffodils cherry trees

the great deserts

the chiaroscuro

2

consciousness awakening   the pillow sinks
in a dreamlake

the mundane puts on its straw hat:

a beautiful day spent in the company of others

3

the snow will melt I will be silent
you will cheep in your tombs the verbs
will roll freely on the page someone
will speak like a god something
will be called a city
or sand
we will seek shelter in a conch

so light so light

almost imperceptible . . .

Bibliography

Amichai, Yehuda. *The Selected Poetry of Yehuda Amichai*, edited and translated by Chana Bloch and Stephen Mitchell. Los Angeles: University of California Press, 2013.

Auden, W. H. *Collected Poems*. New York: Vintage Books, 1991.

Beasley, Bruce. *Theophobia*. Rochester: BOA Editions, 2012.

Bloom, Harold. "Introduction." In *Modern Critical Interpretations: William Wordsworth's The Prelude*, edited by Harold Bloom. New York: Chelsea House, 1986.

Cage, John. *Silence: Lectures and Writings by John Cage*. Middletown, CT: Wesleyan University Press, 1973.

Cairns, Scott. *Idiot Psalms*. Brewster, MA: Paraclete Press, 2014.

Conrad, Joseph. "Preface." In *The N[—] of the "Narcissus" and Other Stories*. Digireads, 2010.

Creech, Morri. *Field Knowledge*. London & Baltimore: Waywiser Press, 2006.

Davis, James P. *An Experimental Reading of Wordsworth's Prelude: The Poetics of Bimodal Consciousness*. New York: The Edwin Meller Press, 1995.

De la Tour du Pin, Patrice. *Psalms of All My Days*, translated by Jennifer Grotz. Pittsburgh: Carnegie Mellon University Press, 2013.

Donne, John. *The Complete Poetry and Selected Prose of John Donne*, edited by Charles M. Coffin. New York: The Modern Library, 2001.

Eliot, T. S. "George Herbert as Religious Poet." In *George Herbert and the Seventeenth-Century Religious Poets*, edited by Mario A. di Cesare. New York: W. W. Norton, 1978.

Emerson, Claudia. *Late Wife*. Baton Rouge: Louisiana State University Press, 2005.

Faizullah, Tarfia. *Seam*. Carbondale: Southern Illinois University Press, 2013.

Frost, Robert. "The Figure a Poem Makes." In *The Norton Anthology of Modern and Contemporary Poetry* (Third Edition), edited by Jahan Ramazani et al. New York: W. W. Norton, 2003.

Haven, Stephen. *Dust and Bread*. Cincinnati: Turning Point, 2008.

Hazlitt, William. *The Collected Works of William Hazlitt in Twelve Volumes*, Vol. 1, edited by A. R. Waller and Arnold Glover. London: J. M. Dent, 1902.

Herbert, George. *The Complete English Poems*, edited by John Tobin. New York: Penguin, 2004.

Hilbert, Ernest. "The Secret Glory: An Interview with Franz Wright." *Contemporary Poetry Review* (2006). Online: http://www.cprw.com/Hilbert/wright.htm. Accessed 2 April, 2009.

Hopkins, Gerard Manley. *The Poems of Gerard Manley Hopkins*, edited by W. H. Gardner and N. H. MacKenzie. Oxford: Oxford University Press, 1970.

Issa, Kobayashi. "[On a branch . . .]," translated by Jane Hirshfield. Online at the Poetry Foundation: http://www.poetryfoundation.org/poem/178443. Accessed 10 June, 2015.

Kaminsky, Ilya and Katherine Towler. "A Conversation with Franz Wright." *Image* 51 (Fall, 2006). Online: http://poems.com/special_features/prose/essay_wright.php. Accessed 2 April, 2009.

Keats, John. *Complete Poems and Selected Letters of John Keats*. New York: The Modern Library, 2001.

———. *The Letters of John Keats*, edited by H. E. Rollins, 2 vols. Cambridge: Cambridge University Press, 1958.

Lao-tzu. *Tao te Ching*, translated by Stephen Mitchell. New York: Harper Perennial, 2006.

Levertov, Denise. "Some Notes on Organic Form." In *New & Selected Essays*. New York: New Directions, 1973.

Lorca, Federico García. "Play and Theory of the Duende," translated by Christopher Maurer. In *In Search of Duende*, edited by Christopher Maurer. New York: New Directions, 1998.

Low, Anthony. *Love's Architecture: Devotional Modes in Seventeenth-Century English Poetry*. New York: New York University Press, 1978.

———. "Metaphysical Poets and Devotional Poets." In *George Herbert and the Seventeenth-Century Religious Poets*, edited by Mario A. di Cesare. New York: W. W. Norton, 1978.

Marvell, Andrew. *Andrew Marvell*, edited by Frank Kermode and Frank Walker. Oxford: Oxford University Press, 1990.

McHugh, Ashley Anna. *Into these Knots*. Lanham, MD: Ivan R. Dee, 2010.

Milosz, Czeslaw. *New and Collected Poems: 1931–2001*. New York: Ecco, 2001.

———. *Second Space*. New York: Ecco, 2004.

Mitchell, W. J. T. "Influence, Autobiography, and Literary History: Rousseau's *Confessions* and Wordsworth's *The Prelude*." *ELH*, Vol. 57, No. 3 (Autumn, 1990): 643–664.

Nuttall, A. D. "The Shocking Image." In *The Metaphysical Poets*, edited by Frank Kermode. New York: Fawcett, 1969.

Oxford English Dictionary (Second Edition). 20 vols. Oxford: Oxford University Press, 1989.

Phillips, Carl. *Riding Westward*. New York: Farrar, Straus and Giroux, 2006.

Po, Li. "Zazen on Ching-t'ing Mountain," translated by Sam Hamill. Online at the Poetry Foundation: http://www.poetryfoundation.org/poem/178453. Accessed 10 June, 2015.

Radulescu, Stella Vinitchi. *Diving with the Whales*. Greensboro, NC: March Street Press, 2008.

———. *Insomnia in Flowers*. Austin, TX: Plain View Press, 2008.

Reece, Spencer. *The Road to Emmaus*. New York: Farrar, Straus and Giroux, 2014.

Roethke, Theodore. *The Collected Poems of Theodore Roethke*. New York: Anchor Books, 1975.

Rumi, Jelaluddin. *The Essential Rumi*, translated by Coleman Barks. New York: HarperOne, 2004.

Van den Berg, J. H. "The Subject and His Landscape." *Romanticism and Consciousness: Essays in Criticism*, edited by Harold Bloom. New York: W. W. Norton, 1970.

Wilbur, Richard. *Collected Poems: 1943–2004*. New York: Harcourt, 2004.

Wilner, Joshua. "*I speak of one from many singled out*: Individuation, Singularity, and Agrammaticality in Wordsworth." In *Inventing the Individual*, edited by Larry H. Peer. Provo, Utah: The International Conference on Romanticism, 2002.

Wordsworth, William. *The Prelude: 1799, 1805, 1850*, edited by Jonathan Wordsworth, M.H. Abrams, and Stephen Gill. New York: W. W. Norton, 1979.

———. "Steamboats, Viaducts, and Railways," and "[The world is too much with us]." *The Norton Anthology of English Literature* (Seventh Edition), Vol. 2, edited by M. H. Abrams et al. New York: W. W. Norton, 2000.

Wright, Franz. *F*, New York: Alfred A. Knopf, 2013.

———. *God's Silence*. New York: Alfred A. Knopf, 2006.

———. *Walking to Martha's Vineyard*. New York: Alfred A. Knopf, 2004.

———. *Wheeling Motel*. New York: Alfred A. Knopf, 2009.

Yeats, W. B. *The Poems of W. B. Yeats*. New York: Macmillan, 1983.

About the Author

Luke Hankins is the author of a collection of poems, *Weak Devotions* (Wipf & Stock, 2011), and the editor of *Poems of Devotion: An Anthology of Recent Poets* (Wipf & Stock, 2012). He is the founder and editor of Orison Books, a non-profit literary press focused on the life of the spirit from a broad and inclusive range of perspectives. He also serves as Senior Editor at *Asheville Poetry Review*. Hankins attended the Indiana University M.F.A. program, where he held the Yusef Komunyakaa Fellowship in Poetry. His poems, essays, and translations have appeared in numerous publications, including *32 Poems, American Literary Review, The Collagist, Contemporary Poetry Review, Image, New England Review, Poetry East, Verse Daily*, and *The Writer's Chronicle*, as well as on the American Public Media national radio program "On Being."

www.ingramcontent.com/pod-product-compliance
Lightning Source LLC
Chambersburg PA
CBHW060341100426
42812CB00003B/1077